# Joyful Parenting

# Joyful Parenting

## Raising Happier Kids with Positive Psychology

Olivia Chambers

**Mindful Pages**

Published in 2025

ISBN: 9789362921291 (PB)
ISBN: 9789362928955 (eBook)

Published by

**Mindful Pages**
Imprint of Alpha Editions LLC
312 W. 2nd St #1834
Casper, WY 82601, USA
www.mindfulpagespublishers.com

# Table of Contents

# Introduction

That takes me to parenting, one of the most transformative & toughest roles in life. It is a journey that can influence the lives of children and a personal journey for parents too. Based on the principles of positive psychology, positive parenting is an approach to PHYSICAL as well as mental well-being that aims to create a safe, happy, and resilient environment, and it is intended for both children and parents alike. In this chapter, you will learn the definition behind positive parenting, what it means for childhood development, and a brief overview of how to implement the principles of positive psychology in your parenting style.

## What We Need to Know About Positive Psychology and Parent

Positive psychology, the academic study of strengths and well-being, takes the lens of What is best about life. In parenting, it means relationships first, building, encouraging, and supporting resilience within your child. The positive parenting approach is shifting the focus from problem solving to an emphasis on nurturing strengths and emotional wellness. Becoming a parent is not about being a right or perfect parent, its about creating a choice for your children to grow but not without you having a healthy and beneficial relationship with them.

Emphasizing connection, communication, and encouragement rather than punishment and control, positive parenting is all about building a strong bond with your child. It encourages kids to practice important life skills like controlling and managing their own feelings, practicing empathy and compassion for each other, and working together to problem-solve. Focusing on what children do, and not who they are, can encourage them to develop a positive self-concept and the confidence they need to face difficulties in life while also letting them know it is okay to fail.

## How an Environment Full of Joy can Beneficial for the Childhood Development

A happy and kind environment is essential for the emotional, cognitive and the social development of a child. Studies have proven that kids brought up in positive settings have higher chances of developing strength to cope with hardships, emotional quotient and solid self-esteem. Happy activities — the laughing, the cuddling, the talking — are the bedrock of secure attachment and emotional health for the child.

However, a stifling or judgmental atmosphere can stifle a child's growth and lead to anxiety, a lack of confidence or trouble making connections with others. Children need to feel safe and have faith in their guardians so that they can tackle the world. Positive parenting builds those qualities in children. This is not to say that our kids should be protected from every harmful thing — it means giving our kids the tools and mentality that will help them process hardship in a constructive way.

One of the most profound benefits of having an environment that is enjoying what it is doing is that you cultivate a growth mindset. Parental emphasis on effort rather than outcome and celebrating small achievements teaches children that their abilities can be cultivated over time through persistence and practice. Having this kind of mindset nurtures a passion for learning and effort in the face of challenges.

## A High-Level Overview of Principles of Positive Psychology

Positive psychology has one few metarule that can help you to change your parenting metarules:

Emphasis on Strengths: Identifying and cultivating your kid's strengths instead of focusing on weaknesses is a wow factor for bolstering their confidence and self-esteem. The same goes for you as a parent; recognizing your own strengths allows you to parent with intention and a positive attitude.

The bond between parent and child is one of the most profound relationships in your life for a parent to develop a strong bond based on positivity. This means listening, acknowledging feelings, and spending time with them.

Promoting Optimism: Teaching kids to see challenges as opportunities to improve rather than as impossible barriers cultivate resilience. Stay optimistic yourself: a child will pick your view of the world.

Showing Gratitude: By being thankful, you not only enhance your emotional health but also teach the same behavior to your child. Gratitude also reminds kids to appreciate all that they have in their life and reminds families to come together.

Fostering account and Emotion Recognition: Positive parenting includes teaching kids about their feelings and how to control and analyze them. Help teach empathy and problem-solving skills that will help them get along with friends and family and more importantly, themselves.

Persistence >> Perfection: Rewarding kids for their efforts instead of perfection helps children build a healthy sense of accomplishment. This helps to overcome fear of failure and nurture curiosity.

## How to Use This Book: Precautions to Change Your Parenting Attitude

It is meant to give you principles of positive parenting, but also some tools of how to implement it in your everyday life. Every chapter tackles a particular part of constructive parenting, with ideas, know-how illustrations, and tangible methods to enhance your kid-parent relationship. Getting the Most Out of This Book — Some Pointers

• Invest Time in Reflecting on Your Current Parenting: Before the introduction of any new techniques; first, analyze your current style. What is working well? Where do you feel challenged? The best way to implement these principles is to be honest with yourself about what your talents are and where you have room to grow.

• Do it little by little: a sudden change in your parenting style is not a positive parenting change. Start with one principle/praxis that calls to you, then expand. But over the long run, small, consistent changes tend to be more effective.

•Give Yourself a Break: Parenting is not a destination. You will feel frustrated, insecure, and angry; but these are signs of growth. Take care of yourself and remind yourself that you're doing the best you can, and every step forward is a step forward.

• Involve your Child in Process of Positive Parenting – Involve your child in process by breaking the news of your positive parenting decision. Talk to them about family values, about where the family is strong and where the goals are. This allows your child to become involved in their own growth while simultaneously cultivating a closer relationship between both of you.

• Iterate: As you start to apply the principles in this book, take time to reflect on what works, as well as where adjustments are needed. Parenting is fluid, and your method may change as your child gets older, and you learn more and more yourself.

Positive parenting does not mean immaculate parenting but building up a relationship and an atmosphere that both you and your child can thrive in. So by adopting the tenets of positive psychology, you are well on your way to creating a positive, meaningful, and connected family life. The road may be rocky so far, but your interactions will be the payoff in an unmeasurable depth of connection to your child, feeling more secure in your identity as the best parent you can be, but knowing that you are equipping your child to grow into the best person they can be and live a connected and fulfilling life.

# Chapter 1: Building a Foundation of Positivity

Your parenting remains one of the most personal things you will ever do—rooted in your values, your upbringing, your lived experience. Your mindset, the curated selection of beliefs and assumptions you carry with you to direct your mind in how to respond to challenges, how you support and nurture your child, and how you view your role as a parent, is the most fundamental piece of every parenting choice you make. Know Your Parenting MindsetThe first step to becoming a more mindful parent is getting to know your parenting mindset. Knowing you own parenting style and implementing a growth mindset will help create a healthy environment for your child to thrive while you grow as a parent.

## How To Identify Your Styles Of Parenting

Since parents have their own mix of approaches and strategies for parenting based on their own upbringings, backgrounds, and life experiences, the methods one parent passes on to his/her children may not be passed on to the next generation. They mirror your mentality, which affects how you approach your child! By understanding your style of parenting, you can better identify your strengths and areas for improvement, allowing you to find a method of parenting that is best for you, your values, and your child.

Other parents are more authoritative, offering clear limits and high expectations but also warmth and responsiveness. Such a balanced approach tends to create trust, respect, and emotional safety with children. Some may take on a more lenient style, valuing freedom and independence but often finding difficult to enforced limits. Although this can support creativity and autonomy, it can also create issues with routine or self-discipline.

Conversely, the authoritarian style sets rigid guidelines with high expectations but tends to be more unyielding and cold-hearted. This method can certainly enforce discipline in the kids, but it may come in the way of free communication or emotional attachment. Finally, an uninvolved style is one that some parents fall into, perhaps due to stressors outside their control, or not being aware of their parenting style. That could lead to a feeling of disconnect, which impacts how secure and supported a child feels.

Asking questions like – How do I react to my child when they do something? is the style of reflection that is taking place. Guide: What are the values and goals I serve to decide my action? What do I want to change, or continue reinforcing, about how I parent? When you have clarity on these things, then you can start to shift how you work, to take more steps in the direction of a style that brings balance, connection and development.

## Framing a Developmental Orientation for Parents

Parenting, like any other worthy task, is about making mistakes and learning and evolving. Taking on a growth mindset — the idea that skills and knowledge can change through work, feedback, and perseverance — turns parenting from a set of rules to an evolving process. Having a growth mindset helps you treat challenges as opportunities to learn, not as evidence that you are a failure, and face those challenges with curiosity and perseverance.

The first step in developing a growth mindset is being aware of your current mindset. Parenting can be a real challenge in showing patience, creativity and emotional regulation. A growth mindset reframes perceived deficiencies into questions like, what can I learn from this event? If you felt yourself losing your patience at a tantrum, think about what caused your reaction and how you could respond differently next time. Simply reframing negativity into self-awareness engenders a feeling of forward momentum and personal agency.

It is just as important to model a growth mindset for your child. Kids learn every bit as much by watching their parents as taking instruction. By tackling challenges head-on with persistence, you are teaching your child that no one does things perfectly on their first attempt, and that mistakes are an integral part of growth. For example, if you try a different parenting approach that goes awry, tell your child, "I tried something new, and it didn't go as I wanted it to. I will learn and practice again.

You should also be flexible and adaptable if you have a growth mindset. If nothing else, kids are unique from one another, and parenting is definitely not a one-size-fits-all endeavor. Having the flexibility to bend and be whatever your child needs at that moment — based on who they are, their personality, developmental stage, and more — keeps you engaged and in sync. For example, when your child gets a little bit old, instead of telling him what to do, you can encourage him to work through the problems and directives independently.

Self-compassion is an important part of a growth mindset. Certainly, parenting is a tough job and no parent is without moments when they begin to doubt themselves or lose their patience. Understand that there is no such thing as perfect and it is not required. Rather, be mindful and deliberate and also know that all your hard work to better and be better makes a difference in your child's life.

Building a growth mindset for parenting gives you the confidence and curiosity to grow and work through challenges. Not only does this improve how you deal with the challenging nature of parenting, but it also boosts your bond with your child. When you show resilience, flexibility, and the willingness to learn, you help create a family environment in which maturity and comprehension can gain headway.

It is not that parenting means having all the answers, it means knowing that there is no one path. Is saying yes to the journey, with an open heart and open mind in flow towards what we know will continue to birth us as we grow. Once you identify your personal parenting style and work on developing a growth mindset, you will have the tools that help you know what you are doing — as well as why and how you are doing it throughout this journey.

## How to Raise Kids with Emotional Intelligence

The ability to manage one's emotions is fundamental to navigating life with resilience, compassion, and confidence, (Daniel Goleman) This includes things like emotional awareness, emotional control, empathy, and relationship building skills. Parents are the key factor for developing a high emotional intelligence. When parents teach emotional awareness, promote regulation skills, and nurture empathy and connection, we provide children with healthy tools that will last a long time

## How to Teach Kids to Recognize and Manage Feelings

Awareness is the first step on the path to Emotional Intelligence. Being able to identify and label one's emotions is part of emotional awareness Emotional awareness is an essential skill that enables children to coolly comprehend the what and why behind their feelings. Understanding yourself is the underpinning for emotional regulation, or the ability to handle and respond to emotions in healthy, constructive ways.

Modeling emotional awareness is the first step to teaching it to kids. When you talk about your own feelings in the day to day, you are giving your child a template. For example, "I am frustrated because I lost my keys, but I will breathe through it and try to remain calm" embodies emotional awareness and a constructive response. By labeling emotions in this way, you are helping your child see that feelings are normal and can be regulated.

Talking about feelings with children also helps solidify their emotional awareness. When your kid feels something really big, give them a safe container to feel it in. Use open questions such as, "How are you feeling in this moment?" or "What upset you, if I may ask?" In addition, it validates their feelings and gives them the vocabulary to express their emotions.

Emotional regulation refers to providing kids with strategies that help them regulate their emotions. Such strategies can be deep breathing, counting to ten, or walking away to calm down. Smaller kiddos might respond better to concrete tools (e.g. a "cool down corner" with calming objects or activities). For older kids, talking through different situations and practicing how to handle difficult situations can help them learn to stay calm under pressure.

You also want to create awareness that all feelings are acceptable, even the not so good. Anger, sadness, and frustration are a very important part of our life and accepting it is the first step towards managing it. You can let your child know that it is fine to feel upset but that they have the power to decide how they respond. If they are upset with a brother or sister, help them to use words to express how they feel instead of resorting to actions like: "I am angry because you took my toy without asking." Instead of hitting.

Practicing regularly is a beneficial step to take! Emotional regulation is something that children learn over time, through practice and with gentle guidance. Encourage small achievements, tell them everyone makes mistakes and it is part of the learning process.

## Empathy and Connection — Value of Fullness

If self-awareness and regulation can be described as the intrapersonal side of emotional intelligence, then empathy and connection describe the interpersonal side of emotional intelligence. But empathy — the capacity to recognize or feel what others are feeling — is a hallmark of human kindness, collaboration, and a foundation for lasting relationships.

Empathy can be cultivated from teaching children to identify emotions of other people, right? This can continue into the daily experiences, asking something like, "How do you think your friend felt when he didn't get a turn?" Or noticing how you feel when something happens in an article or film. Playing devil's advocate with your child these kinds of conversations helps your child to look at the world through the eyes of others, the building blocks of being empathetic.

So building empathy partly means teaching children to model appropriate compassionate responses. Your child learns kindness by seeing you help somebody. If a family member is struggling, get your child involved in small acts of care, like writing a note or giving a hug to lift spirits. These experiences teach them what empathy practiced looks like.

Relationship is key to building empathy and emotional intelligence. How a child understands relationships depends a lot on the way he interacted with parents or caregivers. When you have developed a close emotional connection with your child, they are safe and can explore and relate to others.

All of this requires a lot of quality time and some active listening. Focusing on your child in the moment, tells them their words and feelings are important. By listening without interruption and without a knee-jerk desire to solve whatever issue is at hand, they feel heard and understood. This validation boosts their confidence as well, and helps them communicate further.

Connection also includes helping your child work through conflicts in a healthy way. Instead, use disagreements and arguments between children as teaching moments in empathy and problem-solving. For instance, if your kid has an argument with a sibling, promote listening to their perspectives and coming to an agreeable solution for each that respects each other. Through these experiences, children learn how healthy relationships operate, how to deal with conflict and the importance of empathy in resolving differences.

Emotional intelligence can go a long way — if you teach your child how to control his emotions, it will not only help him cope with his emotions but also help him grow into an individual who can establish and maintain successful relationships with others who are kind beings. These abilities will be invaluable as they get older; helping them make friends, work with others and move through the trials of life.

Through your emphasis on emotional awareness and regulation, empathy, and connection, you are nourishing your child through emotional and social landscapes that can be difficult to traverse. Emotional intelligence is not a static attribute, but rather a set of talents honed over time. By providing your child with consistent guidance in a supportive environment, you are teaching the skills needed for a life of understanding, resilience, and connection.

## Cultivating a Well Family Culture

Family is not just a bunch of people living under one roof; it is a community that exists around shared values, traditions, and the pursuit of the same goals. Positive family culture is the soil in which deep connections, mutual help, and purpose bloom. It fosters an atmosphere where every family member is appreciated and encouraged to bring their unique contributions to the family structure. A strong, positive family culture is cultivated when parents intentionally set family values, nurture traditions, and encourage common goals.

## Establishing Family Values and Norms

The values that represent what the family is all about lie at the core of a positive family culture. Values are guiding principles, determining how family members interact with one another and approach life's challenges. To name these values is to forge a common bond and a sense of direction that will carry the family through the joyous times as well as through the difficult times.

Core family values start with reflection within. Think about what your family values the most. Is kindness a priority? Do you value honesty, perseverance, or benevolence? Your family may hold education, creativity, or adventure in high regard. Once you identify these core values, you need to make them visible and actionable in day-to-day life. If kindness is a primary value, find small or large avenues to practice it whether in small acts of thoughtfulness at home or volunteer and community service projects.

Engaging every family member in writing down values helps to create ownership. Have a family meeting to discuss what everyone feels is most important. This opens up a discussion around shared values but it also allows children to reflect on their personal beliefs and actions.

In fact, traditions help strengthen family values. Their rituals create meaning that links the family across time and generations; they create stable joy. Traditions can be small, like a weekly movie night or a bedtime routine, or more significant, like a special meal on birthdays. These could also be events that happen every year, such as holiday decorating or a family vacation. They help to create moments where celebrating being together and being a family means something special.

Traditions, of course, are partly organic but they can also be constructed. Consider some activities or rituals that align with your family values and will make all participants happy this time a year. For instance, if your family begets education, a weekly tradition of being "book night" where each family member takes turn presenting something they've learnt can evolve into an endearing ritual. If making generosity part of the holiday is a priority, one way to practice it as a family or to make it a value is to volunteer together or run a charity drive during the holidays.

## Promoting Joint Family Goals

Its wonderful what shared goals or even a vision can do for a family, having something to work towards together. Examples include practical matters such as saving for a trip or tackling a home project, or more aspirational goals such as encouraging sustainability or healthier lifestyle. Collaborating → Goal setting and working towards shared targets promote collaboration, resilience, and accountability and strengthen family bonds.

Open dialogue is the first step toward establishing common objectives. Get feedback from each family member on what they would like to accomplish together as well as how to make family life better. And these conversations can surface things that are important to each of you and generate collective excitement. For instance, if one of your kids wants to be outside more, think about going on a new hiking trail every month as a family goal.

After selecting a goal, it is crucial to know what to do next. Divide the goal into smaller steps, delegating part of the task or the responsibility to each member of the family. So if the end goal of an activity is planting a family garden, the children may choose what to plant, while the parents prepare the soil and teach the skills of gardening. These collective endeavors encourage the collaboration that gets things done.

Have milestones to celebrate along the way to stay motivated and excited about the journey. The little bits of success (the first jog, the first hike, the first green sprouts in the garden) remind everyone of the fun to be had working together. These celebrations also provide an opportunity for all the participants in building this journey together to pause and acknowledge their continued progress.

It also opens up the opportunity to teach important life skills and values by encouraging families to set goals together. In this case, a financial target — saving to go on a vacation — helps a child to understand budgeting and the concept of waiting to have something you want. For example, nutrition and family time with a health-related goal of cooking more meals at home. Such experiences both deepen a sense of family purpose and prepare children with tools to carry with them into their own lives.

## Establishing and Enabling a Legacy of Connection

Establishing family culture is not a one time thing, it is a living and growing process based on conscious choices and shared moments. Parents create connection, purpose, and joy by establishing healthy family values, purposeful traditions, and a vision of where the family is going. By creating this environment, children can hold an identity in that culture and also know their belonging in culture making them go through life with having background where they can consider a foundation of confidence and they also include the aspect of resilience methods to deal with life.

In the end, a healthy family culture is a gift that goes beyond the nuclear family, leaving a lasting impact on future generations and the community at large. It shows kids how to successfully establish and cultivate relationships, work toward common purpose, and live in accordance with their values. THIS IS THE FOUNDATION OF KINDNESS, TEAMWORK, AND TEAM THY WILL IN THE WORLD, AND BY EMBRACING THIS STRATEGY, YOU ARE FORTIFYING NOT JUST YOUR OWN FAMILY BUT ALSO GIVING THE WORLD A SIMPLE BUT VALUABLE MOTIVE FOR SURVIVING.

Indeed, a positive mindset is something you need to work towards and it will transform the way you see struggles, the way you approach your goals, and the way you interact with people. Being positive doesn't mean closing your eyes to problems or denying the existence of negativity. It is not about being positive all the time, but rather developing a mindset of resilience, appreciation, and growth that enables you to approach life with an optimistic and empowering attitude. This chapter gives you suggestions of exercises that you can add in your life on a daily basis to change your mind to positive mindset permanently.

## Journaling Gratitude: Creating a Habit of Gratitude

One of the best approaches to cultivating an optimistic mindset is through gratitude. Keeping a gratitude journal shifts your focus from what you do not have to what you have in your life, however small the things are, it helps redirect your mind on the positive factors in your life. Take 5 minutes every end of day to note down three things you are grateful for. They can be as basic as a warm cup of tea, a sweet word from a colleague, or a sunset.

With time, this habit rewires your mind to focus on positivity in your daily life. Taking a few minutes to reflect on what you are grateful for also builds and preserves happiness as well as alleviating stress, which will allow you to face challenges in a much more relaxed and balanced way.

## Reframing Negative Thoughts

Negative thoughts will often be automatic, coming without invitation and at the drop of a hat. Whenever you notice yourself having a negative thought simply pause and question the thought. Reflect on whether it is fact or assumption. You might, then, reframe it differently, to make it appear more positive, or balanced.

For instance, if your instinctive reaction is the thought, "I am terrible at this always," change it to, "I have struggled with this previously, yet I can learn from my mistakes and improve here." So, reframing does not ignore the challenge — it simply looks to your capacity to adjust and move forward, which enables you to make the change, instead of losing confidence and feeling stuck in the difficulty.

## Visioning for Positive Results

What is Visualization:Visualization is a process in which you picture yourself successfully achieving a goal or walking through a scenario. This activity builds confidence, reduces anxiety, and reaffirms that you are good at what you do. Find a quiet place, close your eyes and give visualization a shot. Visualize the end result you wish for, down to the details. Visualize what it looks like and what it sounds and feels like to success and preferably, pay attention to the feelings from success – happy, proud or content.

To illustrate, if you are getting ready for a significant presentation then picture yourself speaking confidently, communicating with your audience, and getting compliments. Regularly practicing this will train your mind to see the possibilities instead of the obstacles, which allows you to tackle challenges with more hope.

## Here is the Reflection of the "Three Positives".

Describe three positive things that happened that day or what went well. From completing a task to engaging in a conversation. And by practicing to take notice of these positives you naturally counter the tendency to focus on the negatives: what has gone wrong. It serves to practice announcing wins, no matter how small, and goes a long way in leaving you with a feeling of accomplishment and gratitude at the end of the day.

## Acts of Kindness

Doing small acts of kindness is one simple but powerful way to reorient your thinking in a more positive direction. And the only human activity that makes us happy for sure, is helping others — this will give you a sense of purpose, connection to the world and it will automatically make you feel better. Kindness does not need to be big — hold the door for someone, leave a note, offer a compliment.

Try one random act of kindness every day. So whenever you do so, just realize what vibe you send out and how does it affect the opposite person. Doing this makes not only someone else's day but also helps you to reaffirm your positivity and belonging as part of a community.

## Mindfulness Meditation

Mindfulness meditation involves bringing awareness to the present moment without judgment. For instance, regular meditation practice develops a sense of calm and awareness that helps you respond to difficulties with more clarity, and ease. Start with a few minutes daily to sit still and concentrate on your breath. When thought creeps in at the moment, notice them but do not cling and do not reject, and cycle back to your breath.

Eventually over time, mindfulness meditation weakens the chains that bind you to your destructive thought patterns, so that you can respond with far more balance and positivity to life's events.

## Affirmations for Self-Belief

Positive affirmations are phrases that remind you of your value, skills and potential. They can also neutralize self-doubt and boost your confidence in successfully handling the challenges ahead. Jot down a couple of affirmations that you believe in, like "I can accomplish the things I set out to do," "I prefer to seek solutions than dwell on problems," or "I am strong, prepared, and clever."

Say these affirmations daily, probably silent, most of the time loud and do this routinely. Gradually, these affirmations will become second nature to you, serving as a reminder to create a positive mindset that will continue to empower you.

Redirecting your focus is a process that takes discipline and time. They are exercises (gratitude journaling, reframing, visualization, etc) that are not a way of life but tools that help you create new ones. When you adhere to these, you can programme your brain to be more inclined towards possibilities, strengths and development.

Provided you understand that positivity is not the denial of problems or the avoidance of pain but the cultivation of resiliency and a positive spirit that enables you to walk through this life with clarity and intention. Over time, with enough repetition, these exercises will establish a mindset that not only makes you feel good but will also inspire and bring positive vibrations to all those around you.

# Chapter 2: Cultivating Joy through Connection and Communication

Nothing else comes as one of the strongest, longest-running connections in life apart from parent-child relationships. The power of a good bond creates trust, understanding, and respect, it is a safe base for your child to fall back on when developing emotional and socially. Creating and sustaining this bond is not accidental and consists of quality experiences which allow for connection and communication. Finding a healthy balance between both quality & quantity time and talking about things that matter can help parents build a connection with their child and provide an atmosphere of love and support.

## Quality Time Against Quantity Time: The Balancing Act

Perhaps the biggest question parents face is how to share time with the kids. With work, school, and extracurriculars filling most calendars these days, it can be easy to feel guilty you're not spending "enough" time together. But at the end of the day, the power of the parent-child relationship has more to do with the quality of time than the quantity of it.

Its a matter of making them count — when you do, not how long you do. It doesn't have to be over-the-top activities or outings but some interactions to make a child feel special and loved. This could be something that lasts 10 minutes at bed where you listen to your child share about their day or it could be cooking breakfast together. Both of these demonstrations convey to your child that they are a priority and that you care about what is important to them.

And finally, but by no means least, quantity time, while ideally less important is still a requirement for getting familiar with each other and building trust. Even for grocery shopping or doing chores, the kids need to know that their parents are always there. Such daily interactivity creates the spontaneity of interaction and conversations that may not take place during structured activities.

There is no clear cut formula regarding quality and quantity time which requires adaptation and a clear understanding of your families needs. On some days, there might be time for a nice long catch-up with extended family members, on other days, it might be a quick check-in, but always including the heart. This guide: Focus on every moments and make sure your kid feel that you are focus and have them with you even when you are doing your own thing.

## Having Real Talks

Healthy parent-child relationships require open and constructive communication. Moreover, conversations are more than monologues, they are not just about sharing information, rather they are about knowing the inner world of your child. The concept of dialogue necessitates a sense of safety and support and your child should be able to express himself/herself openly.

But you can begin by showing interest in what your child has to say. If they are announcing a big accomplishment, or expressing a fear, or something small, sit and listen. Avoid distractions, make eye contact, and respond with empathy. If your kid is narrating an interesting game he/she played at school, you should respond with excitement by asking more questions about it or maybe showing them how happy you are about their experience. This validates their emotions and reinforces the idea that what they have to say and how they feel matters to you.

Talking also provides you with an opportunity to teach and model a better way to communicate with words. Allow your child to express their feelings, thoughts and needs. When they are frustrated, assist them recognize their emotions and where they come from. Example: If you hear "I'm angry at my friend," you could say, "What did my friend do to you? Why do you feel that way?" Not only does this allow your child to express their feelings, it teaches them how to communicate in different relationships too.

Just as important you have to share your own ideas and emotions with your kid, of course in a kid-friendly manner. This allows for trust and connection as they see your imperfections and experiences. Such as: "I felt frustrated earlier because a project failed today, but now as I express it I am feeling more relaxed. This teaches your child that emotions are okay and that expressing them is a healthy way to manage them.

If your discussions centre on discipline or guidance, call on patience and understanding. That instead of jumping to conclusions, or giving quick punishments, try to understand what your child is thinking. If your kid did not do his homework, do not give him a yell but rather ask, "What happened? The other case — Was Something Distracing You? This invites a productive conversation where you can work together to solve the issue instead of creating defensiveness.

Such a dynamic is one that strengthens the parent-child bond, especially when you incorporate these conversations into your everyday life. Regular opportunities to connect take place in simple practices such as discussing highs and lows around the dinner table, talking about dreams and what you want to be when you grow up in the car, or processing the day together in the evening. These are the moments that create a framework of trust to engage in deep conversations as your child grows and encounters bigger issues.

## Keep the Light: Going Back to Basics

Fostering parent-child bonds is an evolving process, requiring time and effort. Striking the right balance between quality-quantity time and embracing meaningful conversations allows parents to provide their child with a safe space filled with acceptance, understanding and love. These interactions set the tone for a lasting bond that is built on trust, respect, and support.

Each touchpoint, whether short or long, serves to strengthen the emotional scaffolding that our kids use as they develop. By being there and open, parents not only develop a relationship with their child but also allow him or her to face the world with confidence and strength. Thus, this relationship becomes a blessing, a fulfilling bond for both parent and child.

# How to communicate positively

Communication is the backbone of every relationship, but more so between parents and children. Positive communication is more than transaction, it is creating a climate of trust, understanding and mutual respect. When parents encourage the open expression of feelings and practice active listening, it helps them create a bond with their children that can nurture them in their journey of emotional growth. It is more than just what you say; it is about the safe space you create for your child to feel seen, and heard and for them to feel as though they have value.

## Encouragement to Share Their Feelings Openly

Children feel emotions, from joy to excitement to frustration to sadness — just like us! They may, however, lack the language or confidence to state these feelings directly. It all starts with a safe space for your child to be vulnerable with you before they can share their emotions with you. That starts with acceptance and empathy — no matter what emotions they enter the conversation with.

For instance, if your child gets angry or disappointed, rather than telling them to "not be upset" or "it's not a big deal," try validating their feelings: "I can see you are very upset. "Why don't you tell me what happened?" Just this simple acknowledgment helps your child to feel heard and reassures them that their feelings matter.

Another extremely effective tool to get your child to open up is modeling emotional expression. Children learn when adults in their life appropriately & constructively share their own feelings, that emotions are a healthy part of life. If at the end of a workday you feel overwhelmed, you could say to yourself: I am a bit overwhelmed now, so I will take a couple of minutes to decompress. It normalizes the feeling, but also how to handle the feeling.

Perhaps the most important part of keeping the lines of home communication open, is to help your child name their emotions. Especially younger kids may find it more difficult to tell you what they are feeling. When they appear upset or withdrawn, try leading them with the phrases describing emotions: "You look sad right now. Is that how you feel?" or "You look frustrated. Do you want to write about it? This practice grow their emotional lexicon and gives them the ability to use words more adeptly to express themselves.

When free of judgment and punishment, open communication flourishes. When children are aware that they will not be criticised or dismissed, it is more probable that they will express their feelings. Always try to respond with curiosity and support, even when their feelings are tricky or hard to understand. By exercising compassion and patience, you pave a way for a strong foundation of trust that invites your child to you in times of need.

So here are some active listening techniques for parents:

Because listening is an integral part of communication, but it is a method that is covered up with a response or to fix the problem. Active listening means centering yourself, tuning into your child's content and feelings, and showing them that you are interested in what they say. The importance of active listening and how, when parents listen, kids will feel validated and heard.

The first steps of active listening start with putting away distraction. If your child asks to talk, put down your phone, switch off the TV or walk away from whatever else you might be doing and pay them a whole lot of attention. Even short breaks can send the message to your child that their words are simply not that important, and that they would be better off not opening up next time.

Sustaining eye contact and body language (like nodding or leaning in a bit) to exhibit your involvement. These little things say that you are there present and care about the conversation. So your body language is very important to show that you are ready to listen.

A good listener uses reflection and paraphrase. Reflection is restating what they have said in your own words to ensure you understand. So if your child said, "I am sad because my friend did not want to play with me," you could say, "It seems like when your friend left you out, that hurt your feelings." This both confirms their feelings and gives them an opening to explain or elaborate on their thinking.

A step further than reflecting, paraphrasing summarizes the basic meaning of what your child is trying to get across. If they share a more layered emotion or scenario, you might say, "It sounds like you feel really both sad and also confused about what happened with your friend." This deeper recognition allows your child to feel more genuinely seen.

Ensure not to interject or make assumptions when conversing with others. Avoid wanting to instantly go to problem solving or advice mode. Instead, ask open-ended questions which make your child to share more: "What do you think might be helpful?" or, " and how did that feel? These questions allow your child to express their feelings and thoughts without being pressured or feel like they will be dismissed.

But it also means responding with empathy – or at least a level of kindness – and not offering judgment that is easy to do even with others we genuinely care about. Show that you are respectful of your child's feelings even if you do not completely agree with the perspective. For example, when your teen is upset about a curfew, acknowledge their frustration rather than say they have no right to feel that way: "I get that you think this rule is unreasonable, Now, let's discuss why it matters. Such an approach helps one understand the other and creates the conditions for an open dialogue.

## The Power of Communication with Positive Intent

Positive communication helps grow the relationship between the parent and the child and helps nourish a child's social development. When children learn to express their feelings openly, listen to others and be responsive to their needs, they develop a safe environment in which to trust and connect with one another, states Parents. Besides allowing kids to manage how they feel, those practices also build communication skills that they can take with them in their relationships with other people.

How to ensure you have positive communication — because it is a skill that takes time to master. Not that we always say the "correct" thing but that we show them that they have a voice that is important to us and that we support them. These small gestures accumulate, creating a reservoir of trust, empathy, and mutual understanding, making you and your child stronger together and better equipped to face the world.

# How to Use Praise and Encouragement the Right Way

The ability to praise and encourage is the most potent tool in parenting. They help with a kid's self-confidence, promote good behavior, and increase motivation. But again, how you praise and encourage makes all the difference. Praise done right nurtures growth and resilience; praise done poorly can catalyze dependence on external validation, or a fear of failure. Knowing how to tell constructive praise from non-constructive praise and being able to use positive reinforcement wisely will enable parents to encourage their kids to soar.

## Positive Vs. Negative Praise

Not all praise is created equally. Positive reinforcement that emphasizes effort, process and specific achievements is constructive praise, whereas vague or generalized compliments are non-constructive praise. Constructive praise builds a growth mindset in kids, which allows kids to approach challenges as learning opportunities. Unlike constructive praise, it always develops a fixed mindset in the children, making them refrain from any risk in life as they do not want to lose their title of being "smart" or "talented".

Example: Praise — Attribution X vs Attribution Y X: "You are so smart!" and, "You stayed with that problem for a long time and it paid off! The first phrase is well-intentioned, as it highlights innate giftedness, but it lays down success as something that a child might feel they cannot change. The second emphasizes the blood and sweat behind their success — bringing home the value of perseverance and problem-solving.

In addition, constructive praise is specific. Rather than saying, "You did a nice job," it would be more effective to say, "I noticed that you colored in the lines so carefully, you must have really been concentrating!" Praise of that sort tends to further energize children to do their best, as it indicates that they are doing what is acceptable. It also sheds light on the specific behaviors or efforts that can reap success, thus making it easier for the candidate to pick those traits up in the future.

On the flip side, throwing around non-constructive praise sometimes feels a little hollow, or perhaps just overused. Things like, "You're THE BEST!!" or "Everything you do is amazing!" could sound quite a boost but can lead them to keep up to too high standards where they are afraid to fail. That type of praise might also be keeping them from being able to accept constructive criticism, feeling that anything that expresses a concern or discontent is a threat to their worth.

And constructive praise should also be sincere as well. Kids know if praise is exaggerated or baseless. Overly effusive praise for small strides or praise for the sake of praise dilutes the potency of your words. Instead, reinforce real achievement or any meaningful step toward achievement, no matter how small, and attach your praise to those concrete effort(s).

## Encouraging by High fives

Positive reinforcement is the act of promoting desired behaviors by rewarding them in a meaningful matter. When used appropriately, provided a sense of pride in his efforts, and spurred him to continue trying. But as more positive things get lost in the shuffle, setting expectations for what behaviour is considered motivation tends to be reinforcing and should only happen so long as it creates intrinsic motivation and not a dependence on external rewards.

On the other hand, intrinsic motivation is coming from within — the intrinsic sense of satisfaction and pride a child feels from achieving something on their own. Encourage this by emphasizing process over outcome in your positive feedback (effort, improvement, persistence, etc.) For example, rather than complimenting the final musical performance, recognize your child's practice and effort to improve with the instrument. For example: "I can really tell how all your practice is paying off with your playing — keep up the good work! in the value of their hard work.

Particularly for young kids or for developing a new habit, extrinsic rewards (like stickers, treats, or privileges) can also work as positive reinforcement. But these should be reserved to be used sparingly and not become the go to for motivation. Need to move to internal from external with development over time. An example might be a rewards chart for doing chores, which could later develop into a conversation about how contributing to the household ultimately makes everyone's lives better and instills responsibility and pride.

One important thing about positive reinforcement is the timing. When a positive behavior occurs, reinforce it as quickly as possible to create a stronger link between the behavior and the reward. If your child shows kindness, say, for instance: If your child shows kindness by sharing a toy with a sibling, say immediately: "That was so kind of you to share, it made your brother so happy!" Immediate reinforcement shows the child worth of his/her actions and drives him/her to do it again.

The other important component of sparking motivation — blending praise with constructive feedback. Success should be celebrated but so should the guidance we can give our children through the challenges. This can be met with positive reinforcement and reframing lack of success as an opportunity for learning. For example, if your child messed up on a school project, instead of criticizing, emphasize the effort and taking of risks: "I can tell you tried hard on this project, and while it may not have gone the way you wanted, you are discovering what you need to improve for next time." That's how we learn!"

Positive reinforcement requires consistency. Such a predictable recognition of efforts/achievements makes children feel secure and valued. It establishes a sense of trust in them and enforces their belief that their effort and actions make a difference.

## Conclusion: Confidence Building and Growth

Praise and encouragement are an art that require intentionality and thoughtfulness. In conclusion, if parents use constructive praise that is focused on effort, specific and sincere, they can help their children in developing resilience and a love for learning. Encouraging them through positive affirmation will encourage them to follow targets with determination, which supports intrinsic and extrinsic motivation.

The point of praise and encouragement is to be a catalyst of self-belief in children and their capabilities. Having a foundation of unwavering support and understanding increases the chances that your child will tackle challenges with confidence and an eagerness to learn what they can take away from the experience instead of just shying away. Your words can help teach your child who they are, who they can be: Choose those words wisely, they will inspire a lifetime of learning, accomplishment and confidence in their own skin.

Boundaries are a vital component of healthy relationships in general and parent-child relationships. They offer stability, teach accountability, and instill a sense of security, without losing sight of mutual respect. By lovingly and respectfully setting limits, your child knows that rules and boundaries exist without being judged, unlovable or punished. It is ideal because it finds the middle ground between discipline and compassion, teaching children the importance of loving oneself and mutual respect.

Put simply, a boundary is a guideline that sets acceptable behavior to protect the well-being of all concerned. Boundaries offer children clarity in a world where so much is new, and most things are confusing. They help children feel safe by providing them with the certainty of what they should do and what they can expect from others. Now, boundaries are not about being a hardass, or taking power for the sake of it—they are about ensuring that both the adult and the child feel respected, and that both have the space to feel like they matter.

Establishing effective boundaries starts with open communication. It is important that children not only know what the boundaries are but also why they exist. If parents take the time to explain why a rule is in place, then the children are usually more likely to embrace it and respect it. If you write, "No screen time before bed," be sure to explain by saying something like, "The brain has a harder time relaxing and sleeping when you view a lot of screen time before bed. Hence, the reason for us turning off devices an hour before bedtime. So, this helps the kids in a way that they do not consider boundaries as forms of punishment but acts of care.

It also entails using age-appropriate language and using constructive messaging. Younger children may require clear-cut explanations and older children and teenagers can be involved in conversations about the intent and justice of the boundaries. When appropriate, giving them the chance to weigh in allows them to feel heard and take ownership over the rules.

A key part of establishing healthy boundaries with love and respect is consistency. Kids are more likely to feel confused, or unclear, about what is expected of them if rules are applied inconsistently or unpredictably. That inconsistency can lead to frustration, or testing limits, or resentment. However, the opposite is true: When parents set consistent boundaries, children get that their parents are serious and that the rules are not up for debate based on how Mom or Dad feels at that moment or day.

Consistency does not equal inflexibility. Sometimes, exceptions are justified, for instance on special occasions or when some defect is unavoidable. But even then it is important to relay the exception in a way that the larger intent with the boundary is understood. An example might be that extra screen time for family movie night at the same time that the no-screen before bed rule would go out the window, but the no-screen rule would be a conscious deviation from the norm.

Empathy when demanding boundaries goes a long way — your child will still feel heard and accepted even if they are being corrected. Kids aren't defying you when they push boundaries, by the way; they're exploring, wanting attention, or dealing with powerful emotions. When parents respond with empathy, they can still hold the boundary by identifying the need or feeling the behavior expresses.

So, when a child has been playing but eventually refuses to stop and come to the dinner table and an empathetic response could be, "I can see you are really enjoying playing and it's really hard to stop. It's time for dinner, and we need to sit down and eat as a family. We'll be done soon so you can play more after. This method validates the child's emotions while also reminding them of the expectation.

Part of respectful enforcement also involves not getting into power struggles. Instead of giving harsh punishments or ultimatums — instead, think about natural consequences that teach responsibility. If the child does not remember their toys having been told to put it away then it could be a natural consequence that the toy is not accessible for them to use for a few days. This allows for accountability without ruining the relationship with their child.

Boundaries are not permanent, but must change as children arise and mature. It may look different for a toddler than it would for a teenager. Children grow, they can handle more freedom and responsibility, and parents can adjust the boundaries to suit. This flexibility also honors the child's burgeoning autonomy and reinforces trust, respect and understanding between parent and child.

This is especially important with older children. Collaborative boundary-setting promotes respect—and less resistance—from teens, who are cultivating their independence. Instead of dictating curfew times, say something like, "What time do you think is reasonable to be home on weekends and why? This conversation helps teenagers to feel heard and at the same time makes sure that the boundaries that have been agreed upon are very much a product that relates to safety and respect for each other.

Loving boundaries are honouring the relationship over the rule. And even though boundaries are ideal, this should NOT be at the cost of your child feeling safe, and connected to you. It takes the fine line of authority and compassion. But when boundaries are enforced from a place of care and respect, children learn to associate boundaries with love, not control.

Your tone, body language, and attitude will convey more than your actual words when it comes to the way people "hear" boundaries. Calmness and kindness, even while discussing problematic behavior, helps to reinforce that the limit is based in love. Don't use shaming or belittling language — it destroys trust and self-esteem. Instead, direct your kid to comprehend, and improve.

Loving and respectful parents set boundaries because they teach children important life lessons, self-control, responsibility, and empathy. These lessons last far beyond childhood, guiding them through relationship dynamics, how to work through challenges, and how to choose a healthy lifestyle as they grow. If children experience boundaries as caring boundaries, they are more likely to carry the same implicit ethos into their own lives.

At the end of the day, loving and respectful boundaries are about having a relationship that is based on trust, understanding, and honor. And while it is a journey that will demand time, determination, and a certain degree of flexibility, the benefits are deeply rewarding: a firm relationship with your child with a sense of stability, and the groundwork for the rest of your lives to foster healthy interactions.

# Chapter 3: Encouraging Resilience and Growth in Children

Resilience is the capacity to recover quickly from difficulties, adjust well to change, and keep going when things get tough. That they are not born with that being the case, it is a skill that can be learnt and developed over time. Helping kids become resilient allows them to face the inevitable highs and lows of life and turn adversity into opportunity. Parents shape their sons and daughters to live in an unpredictable world by instilling a growth mindset and encouraging them to tackle challenges.

Resilience comes from the mindset with which a child faces a challenge. Having a growth mindset that believes our abilities and intelligence can be built through experience and effort allows children to view challenges as opportunities, not as insurmountable walls. They help promote perseverance and adaptability, which are key aspects of resilience.

Kids who believe in a growth mindset realize that failing is not a judgement of their value; it is merely a part of the process of learning. Parents can instill this by focusing on effort and improvement rather than natural ability. Rather than the comment, "You are so smart," a better comment would be, "I love how much effort you put into that. It changes the focus from innate abilities to process, emphasizing that success is the result of hard work.

Equally important is modeling a growth mindset. The way you come out of your own struggles will have an impact on your children because they are observing you as a parent.

Highlight your experiences battling challenges (and what you learned and your ability to overcome) If you dealt with a difficult work situation, you could say "It was difficult, but I took a different route and learned a lot out of it. I will do better next time! This transparency illustrates for children that growth is a lifelong journey.

A second method to creating a growth mindest is to promote curiosity and exploration. An environment where children are free to ask questions, experiment and make mistakes without the fear of sounding silly leads them to possess an intrinsic desire to learn and solve problems. Nurture their inquisitiveness and encourage them to seek answers, reminding them that every query or disappointment brings them closer to learning.

Being resilient does not mean being free of hardships; it means having the resources to meet challenges with courage and ingenuity. To help children face challenges, we create a safe space for them to take risks and learn from getting things wrong. But parents are not always the best judges of what their children need to learn to cope; natural instinct is to protect your child from hardship, when in fact the opposite is true — if a child is not exposed to hardship, he or she will not learn how to cope with it.

Normalize challenges as part of the process. Do not belittle the issue when children struggle with challenges, but meet their feelings with empathy instead, and compassion. If they are having trouble with a homework assignment, you could reply "I can tell this is really frustrating for you. Let us decompose it and find some strategy to aid us all" This both validates their feelings and walks them through how to solve problems methodically.

Another important characteristic of resilience is being encouraging of problem-solving. Rather than giving immediate answers, help your child come up with their own ideas. Say something along the lines of try doing this instead: What do you think that will work? as in, "Have you tried looking at it this way? While doing so also providing their confidence whilst equipping them with critical thinking skills for future situations they may encounter.

Also take time to celebrate effort no matter what happened. If kids know that their efforts are appreciated, they will attempt challenges without the fear of failing. If your child tries out for a team and doesn't make it, emphasize the courage to put themselves out there: "I'm so proud of you for going for it. What did you like about the experience and what can we improve for next time? This frame of mind allows them to see setbacks as a race without the finish line pushing them to continue at all costs.

One way to build resilience in kids is to expose them to small risks. Be it ascending a higher jungle gym or attempting a new activity, these situations help children learn how to gauge their challenges and practice stretching their limits within a secure environment. These small victories add up over time and they develop the necessary confidence to face bigger hurdles.

And where you can, instil resilience by encouraging your child to keep going. Find an example of public figures had failures before reaching success; E.g. Thomas Edison thousand of times experiment before he succeeded with the light bulb. This makes these stories motivate children that even when the way is not easy, it is still important not to give up, because perseverance, after all, is what leads to evolution.

## The Importance of Resilience

Resilience is not just a skill but a mindset that impacts how children experience the world around them. Assisting them in developing a growth mindset and embracing challenges can potentially prepare children for whatever uncertainty the world may bestow upon them one day. Resilient children do not experience less hardship than any other child, but they know how to learn from it, adjust to it, and ultimately emerge from it stronger.

By fostering resilience, parents are teaching their kids to handle the complexities of life — not just to be successful in school or sports, but to be successful and happy human beings. These lessons are among the most far reaching — teaching a child that whatever stage they reach in life, the knowledge that they have skills to deal with whatever challenges lie ahead. Rooted in resilience, children learn to create lives that not only function but are vibrant, rewarding and reflect who they are and the strengths they possess.

Blunders and blunders are an unavoidable aspect of life, however they are additionally a few of the best possibilities for growth as well as knowing. Children will naturally be scared to fail, but one of the best things a parent can teach their child is how to welcome failure and learn from their mistakes. Parents can build resilience, critical thinking, and self-confidence in children by encouraging them to see challenges as opportunities instead of roadblocks. In the key steps of raising a growth mindset and grip of possibility is being able to turn failures to learning and guiding children through the hard emotions that often go along with failure.

Failure is not the opposite of success, but part of it. The greatest accomplishments of history are just mistakes after mistakes piled up. The first step in helping children wrap their minds around this viewpoint is to acknowledge that failure is a perfectly acceptable, and often needed, component of learning. Children who view mistakes as a sign that they are trying hard, instead of as a reflection of their ability or value, are much more willing to take risks, keep going, and tackle challenges with curiosity.

Parents can foster this by emphasizing the process, not the end result. For instance, if a child does poorly on a test, focus less on the grade itself, but say, "What did you learn from this and how can we prepare next time?". Posing reflective queries such as, "What do you believe worked well? and "What might you do differently next time?" allows children to perceive the scenario to be a chance to develop instead of an absolute defeat.

It's just as critical that you model this mindset for yourself!! Give examples of mistakes that you have made and have learned from them. For example, you could say something like: Recently I made a major workplace mistake, but now I check my work much more thoroughly. At the time, it was really good practice for me spotting details — now much better at it. This transparency makes failure normal and shows children that even adults are imbibing and learning every single minute.

Another important key element to transforming failures is creating safe space for failure/mistakes. Children are more likely to take ownership of their actions and look for solutions when they feel that their mistakes will be met with understanding, not criticism or punishment. For instance, a child who accidentally spills a glass of juice can be encouraged to clean it up and think about how to avoid spills the next time. Not only does this method correct the error, but it also encourages responsibility and a solution-based outlook.

## Understood — Supporting Kids Through Challenging Emotions

Things are often easy to feel when we fail or make a huge mistake: The emotional rollercoasters are strong: The pulls of frustration or sadness or embarrassment. These emotions can be intense and, for younger children, unmanageable, hence they do not have tools to cope with them at this age. Coming alongside children in these feelings is an important way to help them digest what they have experienced so that they can move forward with assurance.

The initial step is to acknowledge their feelings. Telling them that it's not a big deal or to calm down – can leave children feeling as though their reaction is something to be ashamed of. Rather validate their emotions, empathise with the situation. That might sound something like, "It seems you are very upset about what happened. You should not feel bad for this — it means you care. This validation assists children in feeling heard, and that their feelings are both okay and common.

Help your child express themselves freely. Finding a voice — talking, drawing, journaling or whatever they choose — will help him or her process the experience. When they are sharing allow them to listen without interrupting or rushing to provide solutions Sometimes they just need to know that someone acknowledges their feelings before they take their first steps to move on.

After feeling heard, encourage them to problem solve. Encourage them to think about what went down and consider what they could do differently next time. For example, if they lost a soccer game and are feeling down, try saying, "What do you think you can work on that will help you feel more confident next time?" This way, instead of wallowing in the failure, you are moving tangibly towards how to improve.

Children should also be reminded of their strengths and past successes. Reminding themselves of times they successfully overcame challenges, when currently overwhelmed by a failure, can help put everything in perspective. For instance, you could write, "Recall when you felt confused by that math homework you did last month? You put in the work and found a way. I can tell that you can do the same here. Remind them that stumbling is just that — a stumble — not the end of the road.

Providing coping strategies on how to process and deal with those emotions is a very useful tool as well. When children are feeling overstimulated, deep breathing, counting to 10 or taking a moment out can help them regain their cool. As these techniques find a home in their emotional toolbox, they learn to tackle future challenges with more alacrity.

## Failing is one of the best ways to learn and grow

We learn from mistakes and failures throughout our life, and each time is an opening to improve. When parents encourage their children to view failures as opportunities for learning and be present in any emotions that accompany these moments, they help develop an attitude of resilience and curiosity. Kids who are taught to lean into failure understand that it's okay to mess up and that they are not their failures, they are what they learn and how they change.

Ultimately, the goal is not to prevent children from failing, but to ensure that they can face failure successfully and with intent. When kids realize that making mistakes is part of the learning process, they are more likely to take risks, practice resilience, and be optimistic about overcoming obstacles. By having this kind of mentality, we help them become successful, but also assist them in living a life of wonder, growth, and discovery.

## Encouraging Autonomy and Problem-Solving

Is not a huge part of ensure both our children are used to dealing with independence and finding their own ways of solving problems. These qualities help them to be critical thinkers, wise decision makers, and adaptable to situations. Development of independence as parents and allowing them to touch their boundaries but supporting them, when required, as needed. With proper encouragement of making decisions and delegating responsibilities based on age group, these essential traits can be inculcated to prepare children to face the complexities and the changing world.

## But Letting Kids Make Choices

The ability to make decisions is one of the cornerstones of independence. Allowing children to make their own decisions coaxes a tiny bit of self agency out of them and helps them learn to trust themselves and their choices. Encouraging kids to make choices, even in the simplest of things, boosts their self-confidence and (subtly) conveys the message that their opinions and desires are important.

So choose the simple everyday decisions first. They decide that they will be wearing a blue T-shirt that day, that they will eat a apple as a snack, or that the book will be read before sleeping. Decisions like these might not seem like a lot, but they give children a sense of autonomy and self-worth. As they mature, the decisions may become more complicated: what extra-curricular activities to take, how to organize their homework schedule, what to do for the weekend. Such activities instill in children the importance of evaluating choices, anticipating results, and owning the decisions they make.

Your kids have to have some freedom in making their own choices, but just as important is creating frameworks and guidelines. This is especially true for younger children, who may be overwhelmed by too many options. Presenting a few options — "For a snack, do you want apples or bananas?" This seperates the end-outcome decision but still helps create independence from the choices made by the person with the IEP.

Parents must also learn the necessity of allowing their children to experience the natural consequences of their decisions. Feeling cold is a wonderful lesson in preparedness and responsibility; if a child avoids wearing a coat on a cold day, that is their decision. If approached with empathy and compassion, these experiences can help children learn to take stock of their choices and learn through them without the fear of being judged or too closely monitored.

It can be tricky to not take over, but help children to make decisions. Instead of telling them what to do — ask questions that make them ponder: "What do you think is going to happen if you go with this option?" or "What are you thinking about this option? This not only cultivates independence but also reinforces analytical and solution-finding capacity.

## Assigning Responsibility That Is Appropriate For Each Age

One of the best tools we have to encourage independence and problem-solving is assigning responsibilities. Responsibility promotes a sense of contribution and builds competence, while also laying the foundation for developing useful skills. Set Age-Appropriate Responsibilities The trick is to give them a task that is suitable for their age and level of development so that they don't feel overwhelmed but leave the field a bit challenging.

With younger children, they may need to do simpler things like pick up toys, water plants or help set the table. These tasks can be learned organization and cooperation and the children can feel happy to contribute to the household. Parents can gamify these tasks or provide praise for completing them to make them more engaging.

The older the children get, the larger the actions that can be assigned, but the small duties are still necessary – learn responsibility! Big kids can help with household tasks like laundry, cooking simple meals, or grocery shopping. Taking those responsibilities teaches them a basic life skill and a sense of achievement and independence.

This is especially useful for teenagers who need the real-life challenges represented through responsibilities. Whether it be a weekly allowance that they manage, going to write their own study schedule, or helping out with family projects, they are picking up time management, financial literacy, and teamwork skills. These experiences build self-sufficiency and responsibility, which serve as preparation for adulthood.

With delegation, communicating expectations is also key. Identify its purpose and how it serves the family or community. Saying something like, "We all clean our house together so that we have a comfortable place to live, where we can take care of each other" puts this in context for a child to understand the bigger picture.

Encouraging children to be responsible — that plays an important role in developing their confidence. Allow them to fumble and learn, but be there to guide without stepping in too soon. For example, if a kid is trying out cooking, give them the space to measure out ingredients or follow a recipe without interruption or intervention when safety is not at risk. These moments of encouragement and perseverance reinforce the belief that they will be able to solve such challenges.

## Striking A Balance Between Freedom And Guidance

This requires allowing freedom but also giving advice to find the upper level of support. Kids respond well when parents trust them to make choices and to accept responsibilities, while also letting them know that in times of trouble, mommy and daddy have their back. This balance allows them to feel secure while they explore their autonomy.

Prompt your child to think back on what they learned from experiences and commend the work they put in, irrespective of the results. Recognise the effort and thought that went into overcoming a challenge or competing a task, and use failure as a chance to develop resilience. This allows for an atmosphere where growth & learning are prioritized more than perfection.

In the end, raising independent, problem-solving children is about equipping your child to tackle life with competence, flexibility, and resolve. When you let them decide and take ownership then you empower them to trust their own capabilities and face the challenge with curiosity and perseverance. And these skills will help them in childhood and in lifelong to live a successful and happy life.

## Exercises to help kids develop resilience

Resilience means that you can adapt to and recover from challenges, setbacks, or adversity. This is an important skill for children to have, as it helps them prepare for the inevitable fluctuations of life with self-assurance and a hopeful perspective. Although part of resilience is naturally developed with experience, there are purposeful activities and exercises that can help parents and caregivers nurture resilience. Exercises like these contribute to creating emotional awareness, problem-solving skills, and a growth mindset within children to help build resilience for life.

## Fostering Emotional Awareness

Emotional awareness is the first step to establishing a bedrock of resilience—being able to identify and name your own feelings. When children learn to recognize and label their emotions, it helps them to be able to effectively process those emotions and respond to challenges in a constructive way. A great example is the "Feelings Journal." Try this daily, provide time for your child to write/draw about how he or she is feeling. If they are too young to write, get them to color or use faces to show how they feel. A smiling bright yellow sun could depict happiness, while a storm cloud could depict sadness or frustration.

The "Emotion Wheel" is another exercise that helps promote emotional awareness. Make a fun graph with all of the emotions: happy, sad, mad, excited, nervous, etc. Whenever your child is having a big feeling, help them find the feeling on the wheel, and talk about it (why they are feeling that way). Not only does this practice build their emotional vocabulary, but it promotes open dialogue about their emotions.

## Problem-Solving Skills That Need to Be Taught

Problem-solving is a key element of resilience because if children are able — and willing — to navigate through the challenges they face, they will be able to approach problems in a proactive way. For an accessible, yet powerful exercise — What Would You Do? game. Give your child hypothetical situations to see how they would handle them. You could ask, "What might you do if your toy breaks?" or "If a friend said something affecting/ hurting you, what would you do?" Strange as it may sound, talk through their answers and dive into alternatives, driving home the point that a problem can usually be solved in more than one way.

Another fun task, especially for older kids, is "Brainstorm Challenges." Pick a real-world challenge they are having (like a school project or social conflict), and write it at the top of a piece of paper. Next brainstorm with the group as many solutions as possible — thinking outside the box is a good thing! During brainstorming, emphasize that there are no right or wrong answers so that they feel comfortable exploring different ideas without the fear of judgment.

Resilience is partly based on a growth mindset (the idea that you can improve through practice and effort). Exercise: Effort vs Outcome To develop this state of mind try the exercise effort vs outcome. Talk about the effort they put in, and the outcome they experienced after finishing a task or activity, such as work on a school report, or practice for a sports challenge. Instead of just focusing on the achievement, praise their effort and persistence. Instead of "Awesome, you won the game" you could say "I love the way you practiced and stayed focused during the game".

Another good one is, Celebrate the Mistakes. Develop a habit of encouraging each family member to confess one thing that went wrong for them during the day and what they learned from it. An example would be: I forgot to set my alarm this morning and realized that I should really check my agenda more carefully. It normalizes for children that everyone makes mistakes, they are part of learning and that failing is a part of the journey, not the outcome of the journey.

## Practicing Gratitude

The ability to remain hopeful is what resilience requires, and gratitude promotes a positive attitude. One of the easiest exercises is to use a "Gratitude Jar". Give your child little pieces of paper and ask them to write or draw something that they are thankful for each day. Put the slips in a jar and go through them together every once in a while (especially when life gets hard). To find joy in the midst of challenges it is important that children use a journal to reflect on their positive experiences of the day/week and be grateful despite how tough the situation may be.

You could also share the "Walk of Gratitude." Go for a walk with your child and ask them to observe the surrounding areas for things that make them happy or things they are thankful for like an opening flower, a sunny day, or their helpful neighbor. This is a mindfulness + gratitude exercise, and it teaches kids to look for the good in their world.

## Developing Of Patience And Perseverance

And resilience can mean working, working and working on through the tough times, in situations that last for the long term. One such entertaining and efficiency-oriented activity is the "Tower Challenge." Give your kid blocks to use, or cards, or cups and ask them to build the tallest tower they can. If the tower collapses, prompt them to think about where the problems were and have another go at it. It imparts the virtues of perseverance, patience, and the art of trial and error.

Another example is — Timed Tasks Ask your child to do an activity during a time period such as– solve a puzzle or tidy up their toys. Do not even point out if they didn't do by the book in the time they were supposed to, but just celebrate their effort and patience instead.

## Promoting Self-Care

And teaching children how to take care of themselves is an important part of resilience because if you have taken care of yourself you have the fuel in the tank to deal with challenges. Daily practice: "Mindful Moments" Encourage your child to close their eyes, breathe deeply and pay attention to the feelings going on in their body or the noises happening around them. It is a practice that assists with easing their minds, checking their emotions, and fortifying their spirit.

You can also craft a "Comfort Kit" together. There you can fill a box with items to make your child feel safe, happy — favorite books, stuffed animals, lavender for a calming scent, etc. When they feel overwhelmed, prompt them to use the kit, modeling both identifying and a taking physical step to meet a need.

If you want to build your power — build accountability and that kind of resilience-building thing — up, that's your power.

It is something we grow with each experience, moment, helping hand, and word of encouragement—it takes time to build resilience. Endurance does not happen overnight. Such exercises will not only strengthen a child to adapt and persevere but also bond the parent to the child. With emotional awareness, problem-solving, gratitude, and self-care — you teach your child the ways to face the ups and downs of life prepared.

With such activities, children understand that setbacks are not the end of the road, but every setback is a lesson. Armed with these lessons, as they mature into adulthood, they learn it is possible to change the world for the better with hope, grit and grace.

# Chapter 4: Teaching Gratitude and Mindfulness

On the other hand, gratitude is a simple practice that can transform lives by having a powerful impact on one shift of perspective in life. As such, appreciation is much more than a social nicety — it is a conscious recognition of the good things in life, matters large and small. Not only does this practice promote emotional balance, it cultivates spirit, joy and connection. This article helps readers learn how gratitude positively affect emotional health, how to incorporate gratitude, and how gratitude can lead us toward a more balanced and fulfilling life.

## The Effect of Gratitude on Emotional Wellness

Maybe it is that, the way gratitude changes how we see and interact with the world. It improves your overall mental health by changing your lens from that of lack to one where you see the present and its values more. This reaffirms an abundance mentality vs a scarcity mentality and creates space for less stress, less desire, less suffering – and a greater sense of fulfillment.

One of the more immediate impacts of gratitude is its power to decrease stress and anxiety. Gratitude helps calm the mind and dampen the power of negativity by concentrating on the good things in life. Thanking for a friend who supported you through your storm helps fill your heart with warmth and ease the sense of loneliness or agitation caused by your bad time. Studies demonstrate that grateful people have lower levels of the stress hormone cortisol, leading to better mental health outcomes.

Gratitude also creates a connection between the giver and receiver in a way that builds rapport; Each time someone says a nice thing about someone else, it creates a virtuous cycle of goodwill and support. Not only does it strengthen bonds, but it creates greater levels of trust and respect. But just expressing gratitude for some support from a partner or friend—their presence, their input—can reinforce that emotional connection and call for reciprocity.

Gratitude also promotes resilience, which enables people to see challenges as a chance for growth. Someone with gratitude, when times are tough will be able to see things in the silver lining or the lessons so that the person will remain positive and strong in dealing with difficulty. For example, if someone lost their job recently, saying something like "Being made redundant let me try new career paths and I might find something better for myself in the end" awakens a proactivity mindset rather than a hopelessness.

Gratitude rewires the brain to notice and appreciate the positive, and the sky is so full of backups when practiced over time. It has a long-lasting effect on the sense of well-being because you can stay positive even amidst challenging situations. Gratitude does not mean we avoid talking about the hard stuff; it means we balance by recognizing the good with the bad.

## Integrating Gratitude in the Everyday

The value of gratitude is evident, but it is only in doing it regularly that it becomes powerful. Gratitude can easily be implemented in everyday life; it does not require a whole lot of changes — just small habits and changes in your target routine and being an intentional observer of anything that goes around you quickly cement it to become a part of your mindset. Such small shifts in thinking take place with nothing more than a few minutes of gratitude — I repeat each day s.d.

Journaling is an easy and efficient way to practice gratitude. Every single day spend couple of minutes and jot down three things you are grateful for. They can be as major as a life goal or as minor as having a nice meal or viewing a lovely sunset. When you think about these moments, you are conditioning your brain to observe the good in life. In the long run, it nurtures a mindset of greater gratitude and presence.

A different approach to keep gratitude a part of your daily life is by referring your gratitude towards other people directly. Show appreciation for the people that bring joy and peace to your life. It can be as simple as telling a friend, "I like that you always listen when I need support," or writing a thank-you note for a co-worker who took time out of their day to help you. Not only do these expressions of gratitude improve your own emotional journey, they also help you strengthen your relationships and create a ripple effect of kindness.

Another place where gratitude can be woven into your child rearing is with family routines. An example would be taking turns sharing something that each family member is thankful for that day during dinner time. Not only does this create a positive environment, it also helps children learn about appreciation from an early age. When families practice gratitude together, they cultivate an environment of appreciation and support.

Practices like mediation which could also be part of mindfulness practices, incorporates the practice of gratitude. Take a minute to slow down and think about what you are grateful for, and luxuriate in that feeling. This deliberate concentration gives you the stability of the present and the feeling of harmony and balance

Even the more boring activities can include gratitude. Be mindful of your surroundings — if you are out taking a walk, notice the beauty of nature around you and give thanks in your mind. Think of the warmth of your home as you wash the dishes. Taking a simple moment of gratitude changes mundane routines to a practice of mindfulness and joyfulness.

Coming up with a 'Gratitude Jar' for kids is super cute and amusing. Have them record or draw something they appreciate each day and stick it in the jar. Eventually, the jar becomes a physical reminder of all the great things in their lives, a physical summary that can be drawn on whenever they feel dispirited or need to think about what good things there are to be grateful for in life.

## Final Thoughts: A Life Full of Thanks

Gratitude — A powerful, but simple, approach to improving emotional health and resilience. Gratitude guides perspective, opening heart spaces, and a to serve the soul with abundance and fulfillment, by providing a focal point on the good and positive side of life. Gratitude doesn't have to be something huge and grand that you try to do every once in a while, but rather a small daily practice that can really strengthen your relationship with yourself and the world around you.

When people practice gratitude, they do a disservice not only to themselves but also to those around them, leaving them more sensitive, kind, and optimistic. Gratitude reminds us to slow down and appreciate the value of the moments and people that give life meaning amidst all the trials and tribulations.

## Teaching Mindfulness To Kids, And The Whole Family

With our lives filled with distractions and constant busyness, mindfulness provides a moment in time for families and children to ask themselves to slow down, connect and breathe to find peace in the clutter. Mindfulness is being where your feet are with no distractions and no judgments!!! In children, it promotes emotional regulation, concentration, and resilience. It opens doors to deeper connections and peaceful moments shared for families. Bringing awareness to the present moment can turn everyday life into opportunities for experiencing meaningful presence if we introduce simple mindfulness practices that are accessible to any age.

## Mindfulness exercises for kids and adults alike

You don't need hardcore techniques or hours and hours of process for mindfulness. Short periods of concentrated meditation improve mental health and emotional well-being. Practicing mindfulness can be easily weaved into daily life, for families this means ensuring all ages are practicing too.

A very good place to start is with breathing mindfulness. We breathe all the time, and never think about it (unless we have difficulty breathing). For a very basic exercise, just sit together in silence and breathe. Ask everyone to breathe in slowly, hold, and out for four, two, six. You will realize that this Shakti brings such composure to the nervous system and creates a sweet silence around us. Some children might be more receptive to visualisation, on the other hand, you could get younger children to picture their belly as a balloon that rises and falls as they breathe.

Another mindfulness activity that can be done by all ages is to do body scans. Noticing sensations throughout the body but without judgement — this is just allocating attention, for example, breathing in through the nose and out through the mouthchmal. Here is something families can do together, preferably laying down in a quiet spot. Begin at the feet and up them, inviting each individual to check out any type of tightness, via warm or ease. For kids, you might call it a magic flashlight traveling through the body, which allows them to connect to what they physically feel.

Mindful eating is a fun practice, transforming a routine activity into an opportunity for mindful awareness. At a meal or a snack, ask everyone to take some time enjoying the food with its texture, taste and smell. Have them debrief what they did notice and the experience of munching slowly and mindfully. Not only does this practice increase awareness but it also brings an appreciation for food and the ritual of eating together.

For active families, mindful walking is a great way to hit pause. Go for a walk, notice the sensation of your feet touching the ground, notice the rhythm of your steps within your body, listen to what you hear, and see what you encounter. Remind each other to pay attention to little things that they would normally miss, like the rustling of the leaves and the way light comes between the trees.

## A Guide to Being Mindful for Kids

Kids come ready to embrace the present, but older kids and adults can easily begin to think more about their troubles rather than where they presently are. By teaching mindfulness, they are able to stay in the present and focus, both are qualities that are important in their emotional and cognitive growth.

Mindfulness is easiest to teach to children through play and by connecting them to their senses. One example is the 'Five Senses Game' which invites them to take notice of their surroundings by taking notice of and identifying five things they can see, four things they can feel, three things they can hear, two things they can smell, and one thing they can taste. In this exercise, they are fully present and free of judgment.

The other handy tool is the mindfulness jars. These sparkling jars are our minds filled with water. The glitter floats everywhere in a chaotic manner, representing a busy or anxious mind when shaken. When the glitter has settled down, it resembles how mindfulness enables our thoughts and emotions to settle down. It is a relaxing process for children to watch the glitter settle and an effective way for parents to teach them about taking a break and concentrating.

This makes "Mindful Listening" a great exercise to teach focus. Take a bell, chime, or any other sound maker and let the children listen to it and stop it when they do not hear the sound anymore. Then ask them to explain what they saw. This practice cultivates listening skills and teaches them to listen with intention.

Bedtime routines can also include mindfulness, which is a good way for children to calm down and feel ready for bed. Even a straightforward guided visualization could take them to a calming place like a beach or a forest where they need to envision it — what they might see, hear and experience in that environment. You could say something like, "Picture the sound of lapping water and the sand in your feet." It takes the mind and the body down a notch to make them feel safe, to make them safe and relaxed.

Parents can model mindfulness in their kids. The best example of the value of mindfulness is in your own practice. Throughout the day, take pauses to give them a play-by-play of your mindfulness practices and how it brings you a sense of calm or focus. Mindfulness mindfulnessi.e. I am feeling slightly stressed, I will take three deep breaths here.

## Building a Family Culture of Mindfulness

That is when mindfulness is most effective; when it is practiced as part of family life. When families practice mindfulness together, they develop shared moments of calm and connection that strengthen the family bond. Be it a minute or two of breath before dinner, a mindful stroll after school, or a visualization before bed, these exercises coax us to slow down and savor the current moment.

Mindfulness is not the absence of obstacles or RIGHT in a world where everything is bad — it is the idea of being more aware and conscious in the ups and downs of life and holding things like kindness and compassion for oneself AND others, through it all. It cultivates a sense of emotional stability and concentration for children. For the sake of parenthood, it provides an avenue to completely by present with your children while carrying the loads of everyday living.

Combining simple mindfulness practices and encouraging children to be in the moment allows families to create a space of balance and presence in an otherwise packed world. Mindfulness is a gift that keeps giving with all the practices that not only contribute to the individual wellbeing but also to the collective sense of peace.

## Fostering Positive Self-Talk

How we speak to ourselves create our beliefs, feelings and behaviour. Helping children to have positive self-talk is an important aspect of building confidence, resilience, and emotional health. Negative thinking can wear down confidence when gazing upon struggle or failure. Through identifying and reframing negative thoughts as well as engaging in together exercises to build self-compassion, parents can set children up to take on life with an optimistic and self-accepting mindset.

## Step One: Spotting and Reframing Negative Thoughts

Insecurity starts with a whisper of self-criticism. Challenging our feelings, aka those phrases that float through our head such as, I am so bad at this, I will never get this right, nobody likes me, they do not come out as a true statement. The first step to promoting positive self-talk is to make children aware of these thoughts Awareness gives us the ability to take a moment and ask if these words are true and/or useful.

Creating a safe space for them to freely communicate is one method of helping the child to recognize the negative thoughts. Have your child talk about moments when they are feeling frustrated, sad, or insecure. Be attuned to signs of negative self-talk. So if your child says, "I always screw up in math," then simply guide them to clarify: "What makes you say that? Is that always true or just your current feelings?'" When you validate their emotions, but push against the black and white of their thoughts, you create space for reframing.

It helps us to change our negative thoughts to be more positive and balanced. This does not ignore challenges, to the contrary, it focuses ones perspective on opportunity/growth. For example, instead of thinking, "I'm never going to be good at math," guide your child to reframe it as, "Math is challenging right now but I can practice and improve. This small shift promotes resilience and a growth mindset.

A great way to teach reframing is to model it in your own life. What are instances where you've found yourself in self negative talk and how did you change that? For instance: trespassing in my mind, I said, "I'll never be on time for this project" and then I told myself I've gone through that before I found a way out. I am just trying to take it one step at a time. Watching you wrestle with your own internal dialogue is a reminder of the importance of introspection, mindfulness, and positive thinking.

## Self-Compassion Building Exercises

Self-criticism is a trait of which many people are guilty, but self-compassion is the remedy. It means that you are gentle with yourself when you are going through a hard time. And raising children to be compassionate with themselves enables them to have a much more sane relationship with their own imperfections and errors in judgment.

An excellent practice at cultivating self-compassion is the kind words to myself practice. Ask your child how they might respond to a friend who was struggling or a little blue. For instance, instead of: "You are doing your best and its enough" or "Making mistakes is okay — we learn." I Then guide them to turn those same words out toward themselves and when it is difficult to say those words to facing inside. This practice aids them in realizing that they are worthy of the same gentleness and compassion that they would give to others.

One more exercise is developing a "Self-Compassion Toolkit." Put together a list of things that help your child when they are feeling down or frustrated. Maybe they will compose a list of their skills, sketch pictures of other positive reflections on events that have occurred in their life, or even write little affirmations that say, "I am competent" and "I am loved." Develop a toolkit which they are encouraged to utilise whenever they become self-critical and make it their reminder of how valuable and worthy they are each day.

They help children build self-compassion too, practicing mindfulness. Lead your child through a short mindfulness activity involving self-kindness. Instruct them to shut their eyes, breathe in the fresh air, and put their hand on their heart. Ask them to repeat soft affirmations like "I am doing the best that I can" or "I deserve love and care." It is this moment of stillness that reminds children of their power and that they do not come with inherent self-doubt.

There are also some powerful tools that can help you to become more self-compassionate, one being journaling. Help your child maintain a "Positivity Journal," where they could write three things they like about themselves or three things they did well on a daily basis. This task drives their concentration to what they own and have done and creates a pattern of self-recognition. On the bad days, they will read their past journal entries and remember what they accomplished and what they can do.

The Superhero Strengths activity is a playful and imaginative practice. Have your child picture themselves as a superhero and compile their very own powers (real life superpowers, like kindness, creativity, or persistence upon perlaining). Illustrate their superhero self and write their powers on it (strengths). This imagery will back up positive affirmation and trigger memory for them stocked up to deal with emergencies.

## Positive Self Talk : The Lasting Effect

Cultivating a love for self-compassion to children helps them to be more confident, and they will be developing the right set of emotional tools to cope more easily and efficiently—dramatically. Through recognition and reframing of negative thoughts, they begin to approach challenges with a balanced and constructive mindset. Through self-compassion, they learn to be kind to themselves when they fumble or struggle.

The skills that children develop in these years not only support their current lives, but also create the earliest scaffolding for a healthy, adaptable and resilient adulthood. Children who recognize that their self-talk has significance, and that they can control it, possess a skill for life upon which they can rely in times of disappointment and celebration.

Promoting positive self-talk does not mean pretending like there are no challenges or pushing positivity. It focuses on guiding children to be kind to themselves and to know that they matter no matter what. Encouraging these behaviours from a young age empowers the children to meet challenges in life with hope, resilience and confidence.

## Family Activities to Practice Gratitude and Mindfulness

Amidst the hustle and bustle of everyday life, your family may be missing out on some of the minor yet special interactions that create mutually pleasant feelings. Gratitude and mindfulness activities allow families to slow down and reflect and build their connection. Not just as excellent individual practices for our well-being, but also for a collective sharing of gratitude and presence in a family context. When families come together and engage in purposeful activities, they can develop habits that benefit low stress, happiness, and memories that will last a life time.

## My Family Treasure — Gratitude Jar

The gratitude jar is a simple but important that allows every family member to shift their attention to the positive aspects of their lives. The first step is to make (or use) a jar (or container) and decorate it as a family. Put the jar down in a central location, such as the dining table or the living room, next to small pieces of paper and pens. Create a gratitude jar — every day encourage everyone to write down one thing they are thankful for and put it into the jar. Everything from an exciting family adventure to something simple and free – such as a meal you love or sunshine on your face.

Have a weekly or monthly family gathering with everyone reading the notes aloud. Especially since it helps to remind everybody of the moments they are grateful for — both together while also cherishing the things they appreciate individually. In the course of time, this glass jar serves as a physical embodiment of family positivity and gratitude.

## Present Focus: Eat Your Mindfulness

The dinner table is a great place for families to practice mindfulness together. Slow down, pause, breathe and observe your food before you eat it. Ask each family member to contemplate the road between field and table: who grew that food, who prepared it, the effort it took to unite the family at the table.

While eating, concentrate on the experience of that meal with your senses. Talk about the flavors, the textures, the smells and what each of you like about the dish. When we pay attention to eating, meal times is no longer just a part of our daily life, but a time that we can connect with one another and practising mindfulness.

This practice of slowing down and being present can also instill great values in children. It cultivates an appreciation for the hard work and love that went into feeding the family and helps to build a pleasant association with eating.

## Gratitude Walks: Getting Out in Nature Together

A gratitude walk is a mindful practice that incorporates mindful movement, the natural world, and gratitude. Pick a park, trail or even a neighborhood route and walk with your family. On this walk, invite everyone to see the world with fresh eyes of wonder and wonder. Highlight the beauty in small things—the colors of the leaves, the sound of birds, the feel of the breeze.

While you walk do it one at a time, and share something each person is thankful for This might be connected to nature, the happenings of the day, or the family itself. Gratitude walks allow you to step away from your screens and distractions for a moment to connect with each other and the planet. It not only enhances mood, but the combined effort and mindfulness go a long way in connecting the family.

## Night Reflections: Ending the Day with Appreciation

Come together as a family and discuss the highlights of the day before bed. Establish a practice where everyone mentions one thing they are thankful for and one moment they felt was impactful. It can be anything about something they learned, an obstacle they faced, a nice thing they did or received, etc.

Not only does this encourage gratitude within the family but it also helps them process their day and creates a positive ending. You can make it more engaging through storytelling as well for younger children. For example, the parents could incorporate the events that transpired earlier into a mini story in which the child is a hero, highlighting all the good things the child did during that day.

Evening reflections foster communication, strengthening the culture in which every voice is heard and valued. Slowly, this turns to a practice that is now an emotional bonding system in the family.

## Yoga and Breathing for Families

This is a great activity to grow mindfulness and relaxation as a family. Dedicate a little time for a mini session with simple, all-age-friendly asanas. Start with some grounding breaths, then flow through poses such as "tree," "cat-cow," or "child's pose." Invite everyone to notice their breath and their body and how it feels and moves.

The session should finish with a short guided relaxation: Everyone lies down and closes his or her eyes. Calm imagery — lying in a fluffy cloud, waves lapping on a deserted beach. In addition to boosting physical health, this practice provides tools for handling stress and achieving calm.

## Gratitude Art Projects

Groups of stay-at-home families can get creative with mitten-making and art journals to express and explore gratitude together. Pick a project i.e. a grateful tree. On a big piece of paper or cardboard, draw or make a tree with many leaves, use each leaf to write or draw something you are thankful for. Dewdrops — Regularly add fresh leaves to the tree, watching it grow as a means of visualising the family's thanks.

You could also do gratitude cards! Everyone should make a simple thank-you card for someone they appreciate, like a teacher, neighbor, or relative. Having children write or draw a thank you note helps them remember the act of kindness they received, and emphasizes the importance of thanking people for what they do for others.

## The Power of Gratitude and Mindfulness Together

Both gratitude and mindfulness activities are great for well-being and when shared within a family, strengthens the bond shared between the family members. They offer skills for life—understanding emotions, being present, mindfulness, gratitude—and create a joyful family culture built on the foundation of connection.

Creating these experiences together creates habits that stick beyond the daily practices of family life. This is not a 24-hour buffet, but rather a gift that expands with repetition, keeping each family member grounded in resilience and hope, and in gratitude for the world and for each other.

# Chapter 5: Fostering Creativity and Curiosity

It is curiosity that drives our learning, creativity, and growth. It encourages kids to question, investigate their environment, and discover the world. Parenting experts agree that encouraging curiosity is one of the most powerful things you can do to support positive development. But if adults embrace curiosity and imagination, not only as a resource but as a norm, they can help children be fearless problem solvers, self-sufficient thinkers, indelible learners. Questioning, and creating a safe place for imagination, are key elements to growing this critical skill.

## Questions and Exploration to Encourage

It's natural for kids to ask questions. The questions start as soon as they can talk: "Why's the sky blue?" "How do birds fly?" "What makes plants grow?" — and their insatiable curiosity (as shown as their grasp for everything in their environment). The first step to cultivating this curiosity is to embrace their questions and view them as opportunities to discover together.

When your kid pops in with a question, answer it enthusiastically and involve them in the search. If your child gears the question like why do the leaves change in the fall, ask them what they think, google it together or go to a local park to witness the phenomenon on your own. And this collaboration meets their curiosity as well as models how to search for answers. It imparts to him that questions are a door to understanding and should never be avoided.

Encouraging exploration isn't just answering questions, it's providing avenues for them to learn through experience. Offer a variety of engaging materials and experiences, from blocks to art supplies, books, museums, or nature preserves! Open-ended play — such as exploring with water, sand, or building with loose parts — allows children the freedom to explore and experiment with their ideas. It encourages critical thinking and creativity, both of which are important aspects of positive development.

Parents and caregivers can also foster curiosity by demonstrating an interest in the world themselves. Ask your own questions and model curiosity. For example, you could say: "I always wondered how bees produce honey. Let's find out together!" Kids who see adults being curious understand that asking questions and learning to find the answers is part of the human experience.

Like the questions, which they may ask one after the other — just at least be patient with their inquiries. Do not brush them off with, "Because I said so" or "It is what it is." Validate their sense of wonder with something like "That's a great question" or "Let's find out together!" This method boosts their belief and makes them continue to explore.

## A Space to Be Creative and Be Imaginative

In fact, at the core of curiosity is imagination. It enables children to imagine beyond what they see and to consider ideas in a more artistic and unique fashion. A safe space for imagination gives freedom, and allows children to express themselves, experiment, and dream without fear of judgment or failure.

Storytelling is one of the ways to develop imagination. Help children to create their own stories, with their own characters and their own ideas. You might prompt a storyline together, then leave the next part up to them. This not only cultivates creativity, but also assists in language development, emotional expression and problem-solving skills of children. It creates a safe container to express for ideas and feelings in a manner that feels playful and even empowering.

This is another great way to encourage imagination, through artistic activities. Provide kids with lots of material (such as paper, paints, clay, garbage material, etc) and let them create Don't give them strict guidelines or outcomes — let their creativity flow. Commend their efforts and creativity, emphasizing process as opposed to product. This freedom allows them to explore and gain confidence in their thoughts.

Imaginative development is further enhanced through role-playing and pretend play. Give them props like costumes, toy tools, or household items and let them make their own scenes. Whether they are pretending to run a store, building a rocket ship, or exploring the jungle, all of these play activities reinforce problem solving, teamwork, and empathy.

However, if, perhaps with the help of a creative architect or interior designers, strict compartments will also be created to accommodate and maximize the physiology and think of the enhancement of imagination. Discover a place in your home or classroom that could be a 'curiosity corner' — a space that contains interesting things like books, puzzles, art supplies, or pieces of nature such as shells or rocks. It provides a contained place for kids to play, dream and tinker freely.

This means not only providing the time and space for imaginative thinking to thrive, but also providing opportunities to take risks and try out new ideas, as well as the freedom to be unafraid to fail. When their tower of blocks tumbles down, or their science experiment fails to go as planned, encourage them to reflect and go again. Reassure them that making mistakes is all part of the process of learning and it is their eagerness to experiment and try that is most important.

## Curiosity — What a Difference it Makes over a Lifetime

Giving children the freedom to ask questions and explore and imagine, not only helps them understand the world better but also helps them create their identity. By recognizing challenges as opportunities for learning, curiosity cultivates resilience in children. This promotes empathy because they are looking at other ways of thinking and what could be. In fact, it promotes academic achievement, as inquiring learners are more involved and driven to learn.

Fostering curiosity is a gift that pays dividends well into adulthood. And maintaining a sense of wonder makes adults more flexible, agile, and prepared for a world that is changing at a furious pace. Through open-ended questions and an imaginative environment, parents and caregivers allow for a lifetime of growth, creativity, and fulfillment.

After all, curiosity is a gift; a spark with which we ignight our journey through discovery and connection. If we all embrace it in ourselves and our children, we will have a world where learning is a joyful, lifelong pursuit rather than a series of dreaded tasks.

## Help Creative Expression

Creativity is an essential part of a child's growth, as it nurtures critical thinking, adept problem-solving, and self-expression. Creative expression involves providing children with the tools, encouragement, and freedom to explore their imagination and create out of it. Cultivating creativity through play, problem-solving tasks, art and music creation, or storytelling not only enriches their early lives but also nurtures skills that will serve them throughout their lives. Creating these opportunities helps to inspire a love of expressing oneself and creating things throughout their lives.

## Activities for Some Creative Play and Problem-Solving

For children, one of the most organic forms of creative expression is play. They use it to imagine alternatives, experiment with their assertions, and discover the importance of being adaptable and ingenious when confronted with a problem. Playing without a "right" way to do it encourages creativity and promotes chances for kids to work on their problem-solving skills.

Creative play, like building with blocks, cardboard, etc. As they build towers, bridges, or little worlds kids can play with design, stability and structure! When what they build crumples, or what they design proves ineffective, they are given a chance to ask themselves critical questions, re-think and try again. It is not only impart domains of resilience but the elements of persistence and adaptation.

Another powerful outlet is role-playing and pretend play. Pretending to be chefs, astronauts, explorers, etc. when children engage in some of their play, it is imagination at work, and they are actually solving problems. An example is roleplaying in a restaurant such as, build up menus, taking orders, and 'cooking' the food, that helps with planning, spontaneity, a connection to others, etc. These enjoyable moments contribute to children expressing themselves and reinforcing their trust in their thoughts and concepts.

Games like Chess and puzzles that require Logic, enhance Creative Problem Solving. For instance, treasure hunts (seek and solve clues to reach the prize) and building challenges (design solutions for a given task, such as build a boat that floats) allow children to think creatively as well as analytically. Prompting kids to create their own rules or adjust these games also enhances their sense of autonomy and creativity.

## Fostering an Appreciation for Art, Music and Storytelling

Art, music, and storytelling are sartorial creative expressions that enable humans — and children, especially — to explore their feelings, thoughts, and worldview. By introducing these activities at such an early age, you can nurture a genuine love for creativity and give your children the opportunity to refine skills that only beauty or art can hone and strengthen the mind and heart.

Art allows kids to communicate visually without the boundaries of words. You let them draw, paint, or even mold some clay; these simple activities convey their imagination into physical objects. Giving them access to numerous resources like crayons, markers, watercolors, and recycled objects allows them to play around with different mediums and figure out what they like best. It's not about making "perfect" art — it's about process, and finding beauty in their own individual style here long before they master their artistic craft.

Besides that, music is also a great form of creative expression. Children can make music by singing, dancing, or playing an instrument, and the feeling and movement of music can bring a great deal of happiness into the home. Even very simple things like clapping to a beat or singing songs together helps your child learn the music, and perhaps more importantly, the love of music and self-expression. When children are a little older, exposing them to various genres and styles of music from around the world can expand their horizons and fuel their creativity.

Telling Stories Makes Use of a Childs Imagination and Word Skills. They organize their thoughts and put their ideas into words by telling stories, through books, or bed time stories, or acting out a scene. When children can imagine their own stories—characters, places, plots—they begin to think in stories and build their own communication skills. Using props such as puppets, costumes or common household items can enhance storytelling.

For families, sharing the experience of telling a story can also develop a practicing working bond. Work together to create a story, with each speaker contributing a sentence or concept to the narrative. Not just does this activity encourage creativity, but over time she learns the value of collaborating and mine-shaping as a team.

## Fostering an Enviorment that Iterates Creativity

The most important thing you can do to foster creative expression is to foster an environment in which children will feel safe expressing their ideas without fear of criticism or failure. Celebrate the efforts and experience of creating instead of celebrating the final product. To illustrate, when a child creates an abstract painting, we shouldnagma3t askWha792M/572/ug547424g5195 it14763? For example, say "I really like your color choices! "Can you talk me through your painting? This method also affirms their creativity and invites them to express their ideas.

Create a space for creativity — an art corner, a music space, a storytelling nook. Fill it with supplies that invite exploration and keep it available for children to access when inspiration calls for the creation process to begin.

Exposing children to a wide variety of artistic inspiration is also key. Check out art galleries, music performances, or local theater productions. When kids see their parents reading books, it makes them want to do it as well, you can even read the same book as them and inspire them to develop their own stories. Such experiences expand their horizon of what creativity can be and how they can incorporate new ideas into their future work.

## Creativity that lasts a Lifetime

When kids are able to be creative, they learn much more than how to paint a picture. Through creativity, they learn about emotional intelligence, Processing and expressing emotions. It fosters critical thinking and problem-solving skills and makes them confident and innovative to tackle challenges. More importantly it fosters identity and self-esteem — that their thoughts and ideas matter and they can contribute meaningfully.

To support creative expression is not to steer a child toward an outcome or specific talent. It involves allowing them space to discover, create, and play in their own significant ways. When parents and caregivers promote creative play, problem-solving activities, and a love of art, music and storytelling, children grow up with the capacity to approach life with curiosity, resilience and joy. Instead, creativity becomes not only a skill, but a perspective on and approach to engaging with the world, a gift they will share with the people in their lives and with themselves.

## The Perfect Mixture of Structure & Freedom

The delicate dance between structure and freedom is simply one of the many basic rules of parenting. Kids benefit from having the space to spread their wings and learn, but they also require guidance and walls in which to feel safe and to become responsible. Finding this balance prepares children for becoming well rounded, confident, and capable and to explore the world with respect for boundaries and an open mind. Through providing space for exploration with boundaries and creating those boundaries for safe exploration, parents can cultivate the growth of their children in a positive and empowering manner.

## Letting Children Wander — Within Limits

Children are by nature explorers, and their innate curiosity about the world within which they live constantly beckons them to discover more. It fosters creativity, independence, and problem solving by leaving them free to explore. Children that are given freedom of choice and encouraged to follow their passion will build agency and belief in their capability.

One way for parents to provide kids with an opportunity to explore within a boundary is to give them a little time to play on their own without a structured adult-guided activity. Which could mean creating space so that your kids can do what they want to do, to play with blocks or paint or take the opportunity to explore outside in the garden, for instance. When parents say, "You can play how you want to play," they are trusting the judgment of their children and inviting them into independence by offering them personal agency.

That said, just because kids have freedom doesn't mean parents back off. Parents can act as a catalyst by building a conducive environment for exploration. It encourages children to explore more, try something new and discover varying interests. Age-appropriate materials: For example, books on various topics, art supplies, musical instruments or science kits encourages exploration and self-directed learning.

Parents should also be interested in what their children explore and not be controlling. Inquiring without anticipation such as, "What have you been up to?" or How did you make your creation? invites children to think about their experiences and men write about them· This conversation validates their independence while simultaneously deepening the bond between the parent and child.

To give children room to explore also means to let children make choices. Giving them the autonomy to choose what kind of things to wear, what activities they want to get involved in, how to organize their room, etc. And, this helps them to gain decision-making ability on their own. Providing options even among some boundaries respects children and makes them feel important.

## Establishing Boundaries for Exploration Without Risks

Freedom is good but boundaries help to keep kids safe and learning about behavior and its repercussions. Teaching children right from wrong—where those boundaries exist and why—is possible, and it starts with clear, consistent boundaries. This structure encourages exploration with confidence; it provides them a safety net.

Communication is always the first step to setting boundaries. Provide the rules — Parents should spell out the rules and expectations based on the child's age and ability to understand. Such as: "We hold hands when crossing the street because then we are safe from cars." Children will respect boundaries more when they know why they are set.

In order to enforce boundaries, consistency is key. If the rules are consistently applied, the child knows that there are actual limits and they are not negotiable. Lack of consistency and structure may bring about state of confusion as kids will keep testing the boundaries to figure out where the limits truly exist. Through consistency, parents create an environment of safety and security.

Boundaries should also be reasonable and flexible, when needed. Children's capabilities and understanding all change and develop. They are careful to tweak boundaries as their child matures, which respects their advance, while also encouraging them to handle more responsibility. You may, for instance, permit a teenager to stay awake longer or give them more leisure time on their technology, both of which highlight how independent they are becoming.

It can also help to include your children in the boundary-setting process. Empowering kids to take responsibility for their behavior also means, when appropriate, discussing rules and ramifications. This can create a sense of compliance and understanding that might not have been possible otherwise. An example of this is that if you don't want kids to spend all their time watching TV, both parents should be on the same page because if you agree with the child, he/she will follow through better.

Crossing lines should lead to consequences, but they should be clear and proportional. Consequences should be guiding, not punishment. Check out natural consequences where the consequence is directly related to the behavior as this is what works the best. For instance, if a child is not putting away their toys, they may later on have trouble finding those toys when they want to play with them. Talking about these consequences draws the link between behavior and outcome for the child.

## Balancing Order and Liberation

The healthy balance of structure and freedom has nothing to do with a bell curve of perfect quarters for each and everything that you put together in your day but rather the ability to shift variable allocations to your particular needs of each child in each moment. Now of course, it varies from child to child. It requires parents to be aware of their child's temperament, maturity and development state, and providing him with the right amount of guidance along with independence.

This balance also changes over time. Kids grow out of need-for-structure, but not all at the same rate. Persistently adaptivity obliges those changes to help develop the assurance and responsibility to the kid. A toddler may require vigilant supervision and well-defined limits for safety, whereas a teenager may require the opposite — greater independence and engagement in the decision-making process.

This is the key to helping children find independence while also being clear about the things that are never up for negotiation. It imparts the lesson that freedom is accompanied by responsibility and that limits are not meant to constrict them, but to ensure their safety and that of those around them. How can we help our children learn and thrive — and prepare them for the complexities of the world beyond our home — while at the same time keeping them safe?While it's impossible (and inadvisable) to keep them safe from everything, there is a lot that parents can do to create an environment where exploration and even failure can be encouraged within safe boundaries.

## Inspiring Curiosity and Creativity with Fun Activities

Both — curiosity, creativity — are superpowers that will help you learn, innovate and articulate your way to every problem. For kids, those are organic characteristics: the desire to run, ask questions, and dream of possibilities drives their knowledge of their world. With the right opportunities provided by parents and caregivers, theycan be nurtured, helped to inspire curiosity, and allowed to express their creative skills. Activities that are set up for little explorers to indulge in their imaginations can inspire a natural curiosity and pave the way for a lifetime of learning and creativity.

## Hands-On Science Experiments

So, science experiments are still a great way to pique a child interest and channel their creativity. Children learn to ask questions and put hypotheses to test in a natural manner through observation and experimentation, cultivating critical thinking skills. Things like baking soda and vinegar volcanoes, slime, or growing crystals from a saline solution are simple activities, that give unique experiences to do.

For instance, during the making of a volcano at home, you can do an interactive (and memorable) chemistry discussion. Prompt kids to predict what will happen when baking soda and vinegar meet up and then discuss the fizzing reaction as it happens. Such activities are not just fun; they help children treat science as a course of discovery and exploratory learning.

Creative Art Projects

Among the most accessible and versatile tools for creativity is art. Giving kids ample access to provisionary supplies like paint, crayons, markers, clay, and even junk materials allows them to use a number of different mediums, explore different kinds of materials, and express their ideas visually(combining any of these)over a period of time. What I love about open-ended art projects, meaning art projects where there is no "correct" way to create or get it done, is they give children a chance to explore and figure out their own style.

A solid project is cut down an old magazine / newspaper / bit of scrap paper to make a collage. Get kids to choose and cut out images and words that they feel and put them together in a story or theme. Not only does this exercise help develop arts and crafts side, but it also helps develop the storytelling and expression aspect in children.

A creative idea would be to expose kids to process art — which is art that emphasizes the process of creating art rather than the finished product. For example, painting with an unconventional tool like a sponge, leaf, or even a toy car can inspire new thoughts and experimentation.

## Constructing and Engineering Hurdles

Building and construction sets are ideal for matching creativity against problem-solving. Things such as blocks, LEGO, cardboard, and even household items can be used to create complex structures or creative models! Giving challenges like the highest tower, a bridge that can withstand weight, and a model city encourages kids to develop critical and strategic thought.

For older children, however, you can take it further with some more advanced engineering projects — for example, a marble run, or even a simple machine with the use of pulleys and levers. While development through imagination is a huge part of engineering, these activities teach practical skills such as measurement, balance and planning.

## Exploring outdoors and doing nature activities

Curious people can find inspiration from the natural world all around them. Nature outings give children continual chances to explore, wonder and connect with their surroundings. Nature scavenger hunt (i.e those in which the children have to search out for particular things such as leaves/rocks/animal tracks etc.) can help little ones observe details they may have missed otherwise.

Another lovely activity is gardening, which combines curiosity and creativity. Planting the seeds, watering the plants and observing them grow make children familiar with biology, teach them to be patient and give them a sense of achievement. They can create miniature plots or plant pots to unleash their creativity.

Building a sundial to tell time or watching how shadows change through the day can ignite interest in science and the natural world. Such activities encourage children to question and explore their regular environment.

## Storytelling and Role-Playing

Telling stories is an age-old method of breeding creativity and imagination. Question 62: Can you ask your kids to come up with their own stories and characters and places?

A drawer of props, costumes, or puppets for role-playing or performing their stories. Not just does this develop their narration skills, it likewise boosts their self-confidence in expression.

Another family activity can be collaborative storytelling. At random intervals, each participant adds a sentence or an idea to a story, everything making up the evolution of a narrative. It teaches kids to improvise, to be flexible in their thought processes and the enjoyment of creativity in collaboration.

## Puzzles/Problem Solving Games

Puzzles and problem-solving games challenge children to think critically and come up with creative solutions. Jigsaw puzzles, riddles, escape-room-type challenges can be geared towards different ages and appeal to different interests. Simple puzzles and matching games for younger children build spatial awareness and logical reasoning skills. For older kids, offer a more sophisticated challenge with Sudoku, strategy games, or by creating their own board game.

One fun activity is to make a treasure hunt that has clues and riddles to find a secret prize. Every clue has the children either problem solving, decoding a message, or following directions and merges curiosity and problem-solving in a fun and fulfilling way.

## Music and Movement Activities

They can be expressed through the music and movement creative outlet while expanding coordination and emotions.

Let the kids experiment on the musical instruments, even if it's pots, pans and rubber bands.

Creativity is also inspired when engaged in dance and movement activities. Children can make up their own dances to their favorite songs or spontaneously perform movements based on a specific theme like animals or season. They enhance self-awareness, confidence in movement, and ideas through imagination.

## Promoting Reflection and Sharing

Take time after any event to share reflections. Find out from kids what they liked, what took them by surprise and what they gained. By allowing them to express what they are thinking and feeling, they are better able to process the activity and understand the beauty of curiosity and creativity.

For example, following a building challenge, you might ask, "What did you enjoy most about building your tower? "Next time you probably would not... Asking these questions encourages children to adopt the process of learning and being experimental, which paves the way for creativity to becoming a part of their lives through practice.

## The Delight of Exploration and Imagination

By getting kids involved in activities that are inspiring/creative, not only is the child entertained but is learning and developing skills that will help to mold them for the future. These types of activities encourage kids to question, think outside the box, and imagine possibilities, which are important traits at any ripe age.

When parents and caregivers nurture an environment of experimentation and play, they empower children to use their distinct talents to attack the world through the lens of awe. The seeds of creativity and discovery in play create a lifelong passion for learning and invention and allow children to be confident, empowered, and aspirant.

# Chapter 6: Developing Social Skills and Empathy

Scholarly ARTICLE IN PRESS Social Relationships and the Impact on the Stage 2: Family Structure The child second room is indeed a stage vital role in any child being emotional with its and social development. Good peers give the feeling of belonging, promote confidence and help in developing vital social skills. However, children often require guidance to help them through the nuances of friendships, resolving conflict, and learning how to be empathetic, respectful, and inclusive. Parents and caregivers can cultivate these skills by showing children how to build strong, healthy relationships, developing empathy and compassion, modelling proper manners, respect, and open-mindedness, and by engaging them in meaningful social activities.

## Guide Children Making Their Way Through Friendships

Friendships are an important feature of childhood but they also can be one of the most rewarding yet challenging! The onus is on parents to teach children how to form and sustain positive relationships. A great start is encouraging your child to speak about their social experiences. Provide a comfortable zone for your child to share with you how they feel, their achievements or if they are facing any difficulties in their friendships. You allow them to process their emotions and create tools to move through social situations by listening without judgement.

It is very important to teach children about the qualities of a good friend — kindness, honesty and respect. Illustrate these traits with examples from their experience or stories and highlight the value of supporting each other and understanding each other as friends. For younger children, role-playing scenarios such as how to ask a new friend to play or share toys will help your child practice these important social skills in a safe environment.

When conflicts do arise, help your child handle them in a constructive manner. Tell them that relationships do not always go smoothly — and give them the tools to properly address a disagreement. Have them share their feelings in a calm way and listen to the other side. If your child is excluded then they can express that by saying "When I am not involved, I feel disappointed. Can we talk about it?" These skills provide the foundation that helps children form stronger and more buoyant friendships early on.

## Teaching Conflict Resolution

Teaching children how to resolve conflicts is an important life skill, especially when disputes arise between friends and that doesn't ruin their friendship. Teach your child to recognize and cope withWith emotions When they have an argument, encourage them to pause and breathe before responding. This mitigates impulsive behaviors and encourages meaningful reactions.

Help your child see the other person's view. And what if you taught them to ask questions like "How did the event make you feel? and to express their own feelings without blaming For instance, rather than saying, "You were being mean when you took my toy!" they could say, "I was sad when you took my toy without asking." Aligning these two energies brings empathy to the table, and that offers the possibility of resolution.

Guide kids to work together to find a solution, practice compromise and respect for each other in what works for them. These stages, including taking turns, rediscovering a different form of play, or apologizing, help kids resolve conflicts in a way that upholds their bonds.

## Promoting Compassion and Benevolence

The best social skills and relationships are largely driven by empathy. Not only will this help them develop compassion but also create stronger connections with others. Another way to instill empathy is parents can practice it them self. Practice acknowledgement and validation of their emotions. Perhaps if they are upset about having a hard day at school in this case you can say something along the lines of, "I hear you are a bit frustrated. That sounds really hard."

Be empathetic while interacting with others too. Help a neighbor or be patient in a tough situation, and it gives your child a great example to emulate. Describe your behavior so they can learn the reasoning behind empathy: "I'm assisting with carrying their groceries because it seems like they need it, and doing nice things feels great."

Empathy is also embedded in all through playing games with children that instill kindness. Get them to send out thank-you cards, volunteer in the community, or assist a classmate with his homework. Explain what their behavior does to others and why it is important to be kind.

## How to Teach a Child Empathy: Exercises

Interactive activities can be a great opportunity to encourage your child to get some practice with empathy in a fun and meaningful way. Mistry and colleagues noted that engaging with high-emotion written texts or films provides children with the opportunity to step into other peoples' shoes. Talk about how the characters might be feeling and why or how this may impact the story. Questions such as — What do you think that character was feeling when they were excluded? What would you do to help?"

One more good exercise is the Emotion Walk. Put Your Child In Someone Else's Shoes Example, say ➡ Imagine you are new to school and don't know anyone How would you feel? How a random stranger could make you feel like ↑↑↑ " All of these activities are designed to help children think outside of their own selves as well as develop emotional awareness.

Of course, peace will not reign in the region by looking for the incarcerated but only if students are taught respect and open-mindedness.

Respect and open-mindedness are key in moving through social environments. Appreciate Diversity At Home: Celebrate differences with children at home first and teach them to learn the differences. Bring in stories, traditions, and foods from different cultures and discuss how diversity makes the world a better place! Carry the message that everyone comes from a different experiences and dynamics that need to be acknowledged and respected.

Teach your child about how lack of respect can be anti-social. Listening without interrupting Averaging due to some differences Dealing with pure human kindness?

Demonstrate respectful conduct by discussing differences of opinion in a calm manner and showing appreciation for diverse opinions.

Promote asking questions about what others have experienced and what they believe about the world, in a kind and curious way. When they meet someone of a different culture, recommend a question like, "What are your traditions? It encourages tolerance and teaches kids to see differences as chances to learn and engage.

## Remember Positive Socialization Activities For Children

Having social engagements allows your kids to practice their inter-personal skills and develop important relationships. Participation in team sports, group art projects, or theater endeavors fosters collaboration, communication, and teamwork. Such settings impart a sense of common goal working while respecting others' contributions.

For younger kids social interaction is always going to be valuable, arranging playdates or group outings simply provides a less structured, safe and fun environment to work on social skills. Collaborative activities such as games or building projects promote teamwork and shared problem-solving, serving as a basis for healthy peer interactions.

Volunteering together as a family can be a great way to teach children social awareness and empathy, especially for older children. Volunteering at a food bank or participating in a community clean-up are just some of the ways these activities invite children to give back to their community and collaborate with others.

## Fostering Social Growth

Healthy peer relationships are created by combining skills and feelings. When guiding kids through friendships, conflicts, and learning outs what it means to be respectful and empathetic, those qualities will all be carried over into the social world. These not only give them a more enriched childhood life but also prepare them for deeper relationship building in life.

Fostering curiosity, compassion and collaboration in social contexts reinforces these skills. When children interact with fellow kids, they understand that differences must be celebrated, kindness honoured and difficulties to be faced cohesively. Nurturing these characteristics allows parents to help children develop into empathetic, respectful, and socially-skilled members of society who are able to form meaningful relationships that contribute to the good of their communities.

# Chapter 7: Building a Home Environment free from Toxicity

The bonds created by the physical environment of our homes form the basis of our happiness as well as emotional well-being. An organized and positive space induces calmness and lowers anxiety, allowing family members to enjoy their home. Creating a clean, serene environment requires getting rid of clutter, placing the furniture in a strategic way, and integrating natural light, soft color tones, and personal touches that represent the family dynamics. With these options, the home can become a safe haven where all can come back to feel at ease.

This is crucial with children around, given how relevant play and learning quarters are. These spaces must be multifaceted and inclusive while inspiring ingenuity and inquiry and concentrating on a single topic. A playroom that ignites creativity or a study nook that facilitates focus may aid children in growing emotionally and intellectually. The spaces have a functionality as well as serve to add significant value to a home, causing it to be full of inspiration and cheerfulness.

## Family-centered habits and traditions

Family life is built on routines and rituals that resemble a heartbeat, offering a reliable and palpable rhythm for connection and stability. Daily and weekly rituals bind us to one another and create opportunities for connection. Even things as simple as having a family breakfast, reading books at night, or going out on weekends may become the fond tradition that brings people together. In our increasingly fast-paced world, these rituals provide a sense of belonging and opportunities for connection.

Finding the right mixture between school and play and family time is essential for balancing a household. Kids thrive on a structured schedule that designates time for homework, playtime, and family time. Too much scheduling sets kids up for stress, while too little means connection opportunities can be lost. Finding this balance is vital for children, as it allows for not only academic success but a chance to play and discover in their age-appropriate way and socialize with family and loved ones, giving the family a wide variety of experiences.

## Encouraging Cooperation at Home

Each household can become a common team set on achieving intertwined aspirations in tandem with the spirit of cooperation. Teamwork: A very good way to make chores and other things work together and work the right way is to encourage teamwork among the house members helping this way to balance the tasks with teaching kids the beauty of working together. Even simple chores that you do together, like those age-appropriate chores you assigned, can become connection moments and help the whole family feel accomplished. Togetherness creates a network of accountability and help, which is good for daily living for everyone.

At home, practicing gratitude and appreciation makes this cooperation dynamic even stronger. Even the smallest of accomplishments are acknowledged, and that creates a sense of respect and positivity. Saying thank you to someone for helping out by cleaning after dinner or helping out during a busy day strengthens relationships and reinforces the collective bond of the family. Gratitude encourages people to see the good in one another and cultivates a space of compassion and tenderness.

## How to Make a Family Happiness Plan

A family happiness plan is a roadmap to joy and a family bond that stays strong. The plan helps map out a common vision of what the family wishes to achieve together, whether it be remembering to spend quality time with one another or making sure to communicate openly with each member, or seeking to invest in the growth of its individual members. It may include pledges to maintain traditions, foster collaboration and create space for play and rest. Periodic Review and Adaptation — It is important to regularly revisit the plan and make adjustments to how it is captured so that it continues to reflect the changing needs and objectives of the family.

With thoughtful environmental design, meaningful rituals, collaborative work, and a plan for happiness, families can create an environment of joy, connection, and emotional wellness in the home. A happy home is not merely a location, it is a living organism, a variety of individuals, and a community where every member is valued and nurtured in their efforts to flourish.

# Conclusion

Parenting life is deep with joys, struggles and growth. Through the strong lessons of parenting where they will often look back on how they got where they are, they will find the story of the family, defined by the values, upbringing, and love that their parents afford through their children. Reflecting on your journey as a parent requires you to look back to the milestone moments – big and small – that have helped shape your children along the way. Not just the wins, the way we learn through the hard parts, but the way that our bond strengthens with every attempt. This exercise is also not just a way of seeing the impact that you are having on your children but also, acknowledging the grace and fluidity that parenting requires.

The final step of this transition into the role of intentional parenting is setting intentions for how we will parent joyfully moving forward. Parenting involves never being all done; it requires even more adaptability and an openness to progress. Each stage of a child brings new ways to meet, feed, and direct. Conscious parenting is enjoying these moments, creating purposefulness, aligning yourself to create emotional guidance and strength and not so much all the negative things that happen in our daily lives. This is putting their needs first, but balancing them with your own in such a way that the whole family can flourish. Perfect parenting is a myth, so joyful parenting requires doing the imperfect thing (both right and wrong) with patience, laughter and love. By articulating your goals on how to approach those challenges and continue to be a source of joy for your family, you will continue to derive meaning and pleasure from your journey as a parent.

As we think about the final thoughts on positive parenting, this is clearly a method that is going to build children into healthy, happy, and even confident adults. Positive parenting is all about applying empathy, communication, and encouragement to create a nurturing environment in which your children can feel valued and supported. It is about rearing people who have the tools to take on life but are also happy and have meaning in what they do. The path of parenthood may be strewn with challenges but it comingled with some of the deepest rewards. The connections made, the knowledge gained, and the love passed down are an everlasting inheritance, and the fabric of succession.

Take time to look back on your parenting achievements and the growth you have nurtured in your family as you close this chapter. Raising decent, competent, and strong human beings is not just a solidative responsibility to the world, but a unique opportunity too, but know that it is a work of a lifetime. You are not only giving your children a gift in reflecting on the past and setting intentions for the future, along with the tenets of positive parenting but you are sending ripples of kindness and strength that will have an impact well outside your home.

# About the Author

Olivia Chambers is a celebrated author, psychologist, and advocate for positive parenting and child well-being. Building on the success of her debut book, *Children and Mindfulness: Cultivating Presence from a Young Age*, Olivia continues her mission to empower parents and educators to nurture emotionally resilient and joyful children.

With a deep foundation in psychology and a passion for positive psychology principles, Olivia has dedicated her career to exploring how science-backed strategies can transform family dynamics. She believes that small, intentional shifts in parenting can lead to profound, long-lasting changes in children's happiness and growth.

Her latest book, *Joyful Parenting: Raising Happier Kids with Positive Psychology*, is a reflection of her commitment to equipping parents with practical tools to foster gratitude, resilience, and creativity in their children. Olivia's engaging writing style and actionable advice have established her as a trusted voice in the parenting and mindfulness space.

When she's not writing, Olivia enjoys leading workshops for parents, collaborating with educators, and spending time outdoors with her own family. She remains steadfast in her belief that raising happier kids is not just a goal—it's a journey that transforms the entire family.

www.ingramcontent.com/pod-product-compliance
Lightning Source LLC
Chambersburg PA
CBHW031439150726
47989CB00002B/988